100 Bridge Problems

Using Poker Tactics in Contract Bridge

100 Bridge Problems

Using Poker Tactics in Contract Bridge

Mike Cappelletti

CARDOZA PUBLISHING

This book is dedicated to Oswald Jacoby (1902-1984), The greatest gamesman of the twentieth century. For many years, Ozzie was the world's leading bridge expert, poker expert and backgammon expert. I had the honor of playing with Ozzie as my bridge partner several times in the 80's. It was he who first started me thinking about the parallels and cross-disciplines between bridge and poker that led to the writing of this book. I would also acknowledge the support of: Jeff Rubens of *The Bridge World* [Bw], Henry Francis of *The American Contract Bridge League Bulletin* [ACBL] and Steve Robinson of *The Washington Bridge League Bulletin* [WBL] for allowing me to reference several hands from each of those publications.

References cited in brackets; [BW 302] cites *Bridge World* **of March 2002.**

ABOUT THE PUBLISHER

Cardoza Publishing is the foremost gaming and gambling publisher in the world with a library of over 100 up-to-date and easy-to-read books and strategies. These authoritative works are written by the top experts in their fields and with more than seven million books in print, represent the best-selling and most popular gaming books anywhere.

FIRST EDITION

Library of Congress Catalogue Card No: 2003114969
ISBN: 1-58042-124-5

Visit our web site (www.cardozapub.com) or write for a full list of books, advanced strategies and computer games.

CARDOZA PUBLISHING
P.O. Box 1500, Cooper Station, New York, NY 10276
Phone 1-800-577-WINS
email: cardozapub@aol.com

TABLE OF CONTENTS

INTRODUCTION

Poker and contract bridge are the two most popular card games on the planet. There have been International Bridge Olympiads since the 1930s and World Series of Poker tournaments since 1970. World Poker Tour events are now being televised and have impressive ratings. It is my prediction that sometime in this new century, both games shall become very popular events in the world Olympic Games.

I am often asked which of the two games I like better. I usually reply that bridge is a better all around game in that there is more to it, and hence, it takes longer to master. There is much intricacy and skill in the play of the cards and in bidding systems. Poker is a better people game, and many aspects of poker are directly applicable to life – and to bridge.

There have been a few experts who excelled at both games. Oswald Jacoby, to whom this book is dedicated, wrote many books on both games. Bridge players throughout the world play Jacoby Transfers and Jacoby Two No Trump. When I played with Ozzie in the early 80s, we frequently discussed cross disciplines. I remember how he once compared one of my loose bridge bids with loose anti-percentage actions at poker. He helped me see the light.

Many concepts and strategies are common to both poker and bridge. Every bridge expert who plays poker well is more effective at the bridge table because of the extra dimension of knowledge gained from experience at the poker table.

The purpose of this book is to identify and discuss several aspects of poker which are directly applicable and potentially useful at the bridge table. There is no better way to communicate these concepts and ideas than by using example hands taken from actual expert play.

Since all of the example hands are independent units, this is a book that you can read sporadically without a loss in continuity.

PLAYING POKER AT BRIDGE – SPECULATING

Bridge and poker are both thinking games. The main skill required to play either game well is simply the ability to think and judge what is the best action in a given situation. Just as a modern computer has an input device, a central processing unit (CPU) and an output device, the brain of an expert bridge or poker player inputs the situational information, calculates/judges the percentages of winning and losing, and then decides how to implement.

The main consideration in any given hand is to maximize your winnings and minimize your losses in order to keep the percentages on your side. Your optimum strategy at both poker and bridge must also include the human factor. Because your opponents have different skill levels, your strategy on any given hand varies with different opponents. You must learn to look around the table.

Because some of your opponents also look around the table, your overall game plan should include an occasional departure from the normal or standard actions. In both bridge and poker, occasional speculations, a term borrowed from gin rummy, can increase your overall expectations and effectiveness either directly on a given hand or indirectly in a future situation. The effectiveness of such departures can only be judged from your overall long-run results.

Although some of the poker-playing bridge bids found in this book may seem highly speculative at first glance, the various reasons and insights given will indicate the soundness or reasonableness of the action taken. We human beings tend to characterize these occasional speculations or departures either as inspirations when they win, or as temporary insanities when they lose big. Bridge results should be judged using objective evaluations which look beyond a single negative result. This book should help you understand the reasons why a speculation will lead in the long run to success or failure.

One helpful hint which has proven to be very valuable over the years is based upon the concept of fragility or delicateness. These are actions that risk a loss on a number of different fronts. I tend to avoid situations in which many different things can go wrong. I prefer a speculation in which the odds are on my side and one that can win in several different ways. Thus, it is not really gambling – it is more like investing.

SECTION A
AGGRESSIVENESS

INTRODUCTION - GO FAST

They say that life is a game. Or perhaps life is a collection of many games. In playing most of life's many games, it is wise to have a game plan.

Our first attempts at analyzing most games usually involve establishing the strategic concepts as opposed to the tactical – or more simply, the macro versus the micro. Before you get into the specific details of any battle, you should have an overall general plan to win the war.

Perhaps the first strategic aspect to be addressed is whether you are playing offense or defense, although sometimes in some games such as bridge bidding that distinction is not altogether clear. Sometimes, when you are considering action, there are both offensive and defensive considerations, although one usually outweighs the other.

Another useful characterization is whether an aggressive action is constructive or destructive. Are you enhancing your situation or lessening your opponent's – or both. In *Gambling 101* or in *Jacoby on Gambling*, we learn that percentages often favor the aggressive actions which can win in more ways than one.

In poker, an aggressive action is usually a sizable bet (start fast). You win if you end up with the best hand. You also win if your opponent folds a better hand than yours, that is, if he or she does not call your bet.

In bridge, an aggressive bid is usually a preemptive jump bid which moves or commits the bidding to a higher level. That is also often referred to as *fast arrival*. The principle of fast arrival is that a bid can win in more ways than one, and is also sometimes called a two way action. You might be in the right contract or even if not, perhaps the opponents will err. For example, the opponents might bid on, or not bid on, or fail to double.

In contrast, a *passive* action (in bridge, quite often a pass) usually denotes a demurrer or a non-action which in many situations is clearly the best percentage action. This will be discussed in next section. Of course, the true wisdom is to know and understand the difference – that is, know when to *bid 'em up* or *let 'em go*.

In this section, you will see many examples of aggressive bidding. But you are advised to note very carefully the many different variables which give rise to these bid 'em up situations – and the reasoning that make these aggressive actions sound percentage favorites.

SECTION A

A-1 AGGRESSIVENESS - CHARGE THE RED FLAG

MATCHPOINTS	Not Vulnerable vs. Vulnerable
You Hold: ♠ xx ♥ x ♦ xx ♣ KQ10xxxxx	
The Bidding: P 1D ??	

What call would you make?

Since your partner is a passed hand, there is a very strong possibility that the opponents can make a vulnerable game or even a slam! Looking at your hand, it also seems very likely that the opponents have an eight-card or longer major fit. Your mission – if you choose to accept – is to stop opponents from exchanging useful information. What should you bid?

One extremely important consideration here is that the opponents are vulnerable and you are not. This is called *favorable vulnerability* because the scoring conditions are most favorable for making sacrifice bids. If the opponents can bid and make a vulnerable game (600+), you can afford to get doubled and go down three tricks (-500) and still show a slight profit.

Some very aggressive players feel that during this vulnerability anything goes. Pick up your *white* (slang for non-vulnerable) hand and then charge at the *red* (vulnerable) opponents. Note that in England, they call it, *barraging*. Here in the States, we say, *stick it to 'em*.

In the above hand, some players would make a routine 3C weak-jump overcall. But in this white-against-red situation, with your partner a passed hand, 3C is rather wimpy and inadequate. Even 4C is somewhat inadequate because your left hand opponent (LHO) might easily bid a five-card major or make a negative double or even a cue bid.

You should bid 5C! Although it would take a miracle to make five-clubs opposite a passed partner, you are quite willing to get doubled and go down a few tricks, since it rates to be a good sacrifice. The greatest potential of the 5C bid is not the constructive offensive designation of the club suit, but its destructive value; it completely shuts out all scientific bids including Blackwood and it forces the opponents to guess on the five-level. This is perhaps the purest form of defensive destructive bids.

Cross Reference: see hand A-11

A-2 SHEER AGGRESSION

IMPs	Not Vulnerable vs. Vulnerable
You Hold:	♠ x
	♥ Qxxx
	♦ J9xxx
	♣ xxx
The Bidding:	1C 2H 2S ??

What call would you make?

Here again we have the red flag of vulnerability waving us on. Note well that if partner has something like KJxxxx in hearts and out, then the opponents are probably cold for seven spades. If partner has one defensive trick, then the opponents can make a small slam. At this point in the auction, what can you do to hamper them? They are vulnerable and you are not.

Recommended action – bid 5H! After this outrageous five-level barrage bid, the opponents will not be able to bid Blackwood or exchange other crucial information. They will be guessing at the five or six level. If they double you in 5H, and partner has 3-6-2-2, you would probably take seven tricks on offense (that is, lose six tricks) – surely a good save against seven or even six, and about even when there is only game.

If you are playing against average or better opponents, jack it up! If they double you, the price is probably right. Note that this 5H bid is both purely defensive and purely destructive. Your opponents certainly won't like it, and they may well guess wrong.

If you look around the table (as in Section D) and detect that you happen to be playing against beginners or weak players, the odds change dramatically. Since these opponents are less likely to bid the slam, you do not want to get doubled in 5H and go for more than 680. You might choose a more creative approach such as bidding 3N. *See tactical bids in Section F.*

A-3 LIBERALIZED PREEMPTIVE ACTIONS

IMPs	Both Vulnerable
You Hold:	♠ xx
	♥ x
	♦ KJ10xxxx
	♣ xxx

What call do you make in first seat? Do you have any specific partnership agreements as to the minimum strength of a preempt?

In the olden days of bridge, rather conservative bridge experts formulated a guideline for preemptive actions called the Rule of Two and Three, which meant that when vulnerable, a preemptive hand should have trick taking potential within two tricks of its bid, and not-vulnerable, within three tricks of its bid.

For example, using the Rule of Two and Three, a vulnerable opening 3C bid (preempt) which purports to take nine tricks, would contain seven potential tricks in hand (that is, nine minus two), such as AKQ seventh of clubs and no outside winners. A non-vulnerable preempt would contain six tricks in hand (nine minus three), such as king-queen-jack seventh and no outside winners.

One might first notice that the original Rule of Two and Three fails to take into consideration the vulnerability of the opponents. It would not be difficult to augment the concept and restate the rule so that the trick requirement varied with the vulnerability of the opponents. There is really no need to do this, since that rule is of little use outside of academic, and perhaps teaching, purposes.

Why? The big problem with the Rule of Two and Three is that it substantially reduces the number of preempts which your side makes. It is generally recognized that the single most effective competitive bid in bridge is the preempt – as long as the preempts are reasonable, where reasonable is clearly a less stringent standard than the Rule of Two and Three. Preempting generally makes things difficult for your opponents and more importantly, helps your partner compete effectively. The more reasonable preempts your side makes, the better your results.

Since the Rule of Two and Three would essentially prohibit more than half of the effective preempts that your side should make, it simply must be inadvisable to use it. So what exactly is an effective or a reasonable preempt? If not the Rule of Two and Three, then where do we draw the line as to what constitutes the minimum preempt? Is there a simple standard? No. But there are some useful guidelines.

What constitutes an effective or reasonable preempt depends not on any absolute standard but on the relative abilities and tendencies of the players involved. What constitutes an effective or a reasonable preempt is more like a poker human judgment situation than most of the more exact or scientific bridge situations which count aces, points or tricks. Experience and reality have taught many of us that not only are reasonable preempts effective, but more often than not, preempts that are not reasonable, that is, preempts which are sub-par also lead to favorable results.

Thus, the modern preferred view is that at all levels of bridge, it is generally advantageous to preempt not only with all reasonable preempts, but also, at least occasionally, with less-than-reasonable preempts.

On the hand given above, I recommend preempting 3D, unless your partnership agreements clearly prohibit preempting with such hands. Note that if my partner bids 3N with as little as ace and another diamond, there is at least some chance that my hand will provide a lot of tricks for him. One possible standard might be that if your partner bids 3N with ace or king doubleton of your suit, there is some chance that your suit will run in no trump.

The Toothless Tiger exemption: It seems appropriate to mention at this point that many modern aggressive bridge experts have an agreement that if they preempt at the three level with a very weak hand – that is, with a suit that has very little likelihood of running if their partner bids three no trump – they run to four-of-their suit if their partner does bid three no trump.

For example, if you preempt 3C on queen-empty seventh or worse with no outside entries (a toothless tiger preempt), then, by partnership agreement, you run to 4C if your partner bids 3N. Note also, that if partner bids 4N over the toothless tiger 4C bid, then he is on his own, having been forewarned (and even if doubled).

A-4 LIBERALIZED PREEMPTIVE ACTIONS

IMPs	Vulnerable vs. Non Vulnerable [BW 104]
You Hold: ♠ -- ♥ K10xxx ♦ QJ9xxx ♣ Jx	

What call do you make after a one-club opening bid on your right (note vulnerability)?

As discussed in the previous hand, once upon a time, rather conservative bridge experts used a guideline for preemptive actions called the Rule of Two and Three. This hand lacks solid trick taking potential and hence, on its own, does not even come close to being within two tricks of a three level contract. If partner has a misfit, this hand could go for a very large number if doubled vulnerable at the three level.

Notwithstanding the possible dangers, when this hand was considered by a modern January 2004 *Bridge World* expert bidding panel, ten experts chose to bid the unusual 2N, nine experts passed, all noting the danger of pushing the hand to the three level, and the rest chose to simply overcall with the hand at the one or two level. Although this hand could be a disaster if partner has a misfit, this hand could provide a lot of tricks if partner has a good fit, for example, king fourth of diamonds.

The fact that an expert panel chose 2N as the best bid certainly reflects the changes that have occurred in modern aggressive bridge bidding. However, the ten-to-nine vote also suggests that this is a borderline situation. If this hand had been given as non-vulnerable, there is little doubt that most experts would have made the descriptive two-suited 2N bid. But even when vulnerable versus non-vulnerable, the offensive advantages of showing the six-five distribution probably outweigh the disadvantages; no one likes explaining to their teammates why they defended a part-score contract instead of bidding their cold red-suit game.

Still another consideration is that the opponents might play the red versus white 2N bidder for a stronger or more shapely hand (the bluff factor) or otherwise misjudge the auction after the 2N bid.

A-5 AGGRESSIVENESS - BUT THERE ARE LIMITS

IMPs	Neither Vulnerable
You Hold:	♠ Jxx
	♥ xxx
	♦ xxx
	♣ Kxxx
The Bidding: 1S 2N X ??	

What would you bid with this hand? What is the probable distribution of the major suits?

I chose 4C which is essentially a compromise bid between 3C and 5C. With equal vulnerability (neither side vulnerable), it is probably anti-percentage to bid 5C because the opponents will probably double and you will probably go for 500 or more – more than the opponent's non-vulnerable game.

In order to estimate the limits or the safe range of bidding on this hand, let us put your partner on two typical medium hands. First, suppose your partner has 2-1-5-5 with two aces. If his two aces are in the minors, then you would lose five tricks outside of the trump suit. But you would also lose a trump trick if the clubs split 3-1 (they did). So even 4C doubled would go for too much, 500, more than the opponent's not vulnerable game.

Second, suppose your partner has king-queen of diamonds and queen-jack of clubs. Here you would also probably lose five or six tricks depending on location of ace of diamonds, but the opponents are probably on for slam, although they might not bid it, especially if you take up some bidding space.

Note well what your right hand opponent's (RHO) double tells you about this hand. Since your partner usually has 5-5 in the minors and the opponents play that both 3C and 3D are major-suit cue bids (unusual over unusual), then RHO's double usually denies three or more spades or a long heart suit.

Thus, even if RHO has his maximum number of major suit cards, two spades and five hearts, then LHO would still have at least ten cards in the majors. But if LHO has six spades and four hearts, then the 4C bid might shut out the heart suit, probably their best fit. In fact, LHO did bid 4S on his six-four. From my perspective, although even 4C might go for too many, I could pretty well go to the bank that LHO would not pass 4C, though he may pass 5C around to his partner who had doubled 2N.

Note well that if the vulnerability was favorable – white vs. red, when you are not vulnerable against vulnerable opponents – you might well throw caution to the wind and gamble with 5C. Or if RHO had made either the 3C or 3D unusual cue bids, there would be much to be said for risking a 5C bid. In light of the double over 2N which tends to suggest an interest in doubling for penalties, bidding 5C would be like laying your head on the chopping block. And indeed, 5C went for 800 at the other table.

We all like to be aggressive and preempt the bidding to make life difficult for the opponents, nevertheless, you should not throw caution to the winds and present the opponents with an opportunity to simply double you and collect a penalty greater than their most likely potential score. The specific circumstances usually suggest your spending limit.

In the above hand, the opponent's double of 2N suggested that this hand was probably about bidding game or doubling the opponents, and probably not about slam prospects. My objective was to be aggressive, but also to be mindful that if I get doubled, our negative score would probably be compared with game at the other table, not slam.

If instead of doubling 2N, the opponent had bid 3D showing a limit raise in spades or better, then slam would be considerably more likely, and I would risk a 5C bid to shut out Blackwood and other slam moves.

A-6 THE OLD, THE NEW, AND THE BLUE

Rubber Bridge	Both Vulnerable [1932 World Olympics]
You Hold: ♠ AK10xxx2 ♥ AK ♦ AQx ♣ x	
The Bidding: 1S P 2S P 3D P 3S P ??	

What would you bid if your partner's 3S bid could have as little as ♠QJx ♥xxx ♦xxx ♣QJxx? In modern bridge, responder might have bid 1N with a very minimal 2S response.

When this hand was first given by Eli Culbertson in the first World Bridge Olympiad in 1932, responder's actual hand was ♠QJ43 ♥xxx ♦9xx ♣A10x, and the par contract to reach was 6S. Culbertson's recommended auction, the old auction, was essentially 2S, 3S, 6S. The opening 2S bid was strong (in 1932, all opening two-bids were strong) and 3S was a medium response showing at least one trick. 2N would have been negative, and three-of-a-suit would have been positive showing at least one-and-one-half tricks. 6S clearly should have good play.

1932 was the first big year of expansion for contract bridge. Invented on Harold Vanderbilt's yacht, bridge had been born into royalty in the mid-twenties. It then stalled, with everything else, during the Great Depression and Prohibition. Oswald Jacoby, to whom this book is dedicated, was on the team that won the first Asbury Cup in Asbury Park, New Jersey, which several years later was renamed the Spingold Cup; one of the three most prestigious annual events in bridge. Nate Spingold was one of the first presidents of the organization that eventually became the American Contract Bridge League.

Almost fifty years later, my wife and I played this same hand which had been resurrected by National ACBL Director Jerry Machlin for the annual bridge party/par contest held at the State Department in Washington, D.C. Our bidding (the new) was 2C (strong, artificial and forcing), 2H (step response showed either one ace or two kings), 2S (natural, game forcing), 3S (at least honor third or four card support), 4C (anything else?), 4S (nothing else), 6S. Note that although we ended up in the same contract, our modern control showing auction yielded a more accurate picture of responder's hand than the original simple Culbertson auction.

So what about the bidding problem (the blue) as given above?

What I best remember about this hand is that at the State Department par contest, Jerry Machlin asked me to chair a protest committee where a little old lady was being accused of taking advantage of her partner's hesitation before making the 3S bid (negative). After the slow 3S bid, the little old lady (LOL) holding the big hand, bid an aggressive 4N Blackwood, found out that her partner indeed had an ace and bid 6S. Their opponents claimed that because of the prolonged thought before bidding 3S, it was clear that her partner held more than a rank minimum.

Our three-man committee ruled that because the LOL had chosen to open the hand 1S (instead of a strong two-bid), she apparently was a beginner and was more likely to be bidding randomly rather than taking advantage of a subtlety. All roads led to Rome.

The hand is an interesting par-play problem in 6S with king of clubs lead. See if you can get both play pars.

♠ QJ43
♥ xxx
♦ 9xx
♣ A10x

♠ AK10xxx2
♥ AK
♦ AQx
♣ x

Solution: Win ace and ruff a club. Note that you have three entries to dummy.

Strip hands of hearts, then play 10 of clubs from dummy. If right hand opponent does not cover (with club jack), pitch small diamond and claim (par one). Left hand opponent must lead into your diamonds or give you a ruff-sluff. If right hand opponent covers ten of clubs, ruff it and lead small diamond toward nine. If LHO has both jack and ten of diamonds, then he will be end played as above (par two).

Left hand opponent held: ♠x ♥xxxx ♦KJ10x ♣KQ98

A-7 WHAT A DIFFERENCE A LEVEL MAKES

IMPs	Not Vulnerable vs. Vulnerable
You Hold: ♠ 108xx	
♥ x	
♦ J109x	
♣ J98x	
The Bidding: 1S X ??	

What call would you make?

Here is what seemed to be a rather innocuous bidding situation – but the choice of bids led to a huge thirteen IMP slam swing. At one table, the above hand bid a mere 2S. At the other table, our partners bid a much more aggressive and effective 3S preempt. Note that if partner has a normal 12-14 point opening bid, it is quite likely that the opponents would be able to make a vulnerable game in hearts. With four trumps and a singleton, it is very unlikely that 3S would go for more than 500 if doubled for penalty.

Let's look at what actually happened at both tables:

North
♠Kxx
♥xxx
♦Qxx
♣Q7xx

West
♠ 108xx
♥ x
♦ J109x
♣ J98x

East
♠ AQJxxx
♥ J109
♦ x
♣ Kxx

South
♠ --
♥ AKQxxx
♦ AKxxx
♣ A10

The two auctions:

1S	X	3S	P
P	4S	P	5C
P	5H	P	P
P			

1S	X	2S	3C
P	3S	P	3N
P	6H	P	P
P			

At the first table, the 3S preempt left north with no good bid. When his partner showed a monster, north judged that his king of spades would not be valuable and that slam was unlikely.

At the second table, the 2S raise allowed north to make the 3C free bid, showing 6-9 points, which was all the encouragement that south needed to bid a slam. South was thinking about grand slams before hearing the 3N bid.

With normal splits, 6H would be easy. But because of the bad splits, south had to take a rather advanced line of play to make 6H. The three of spades was led (third best from an even number) which gave south an excellent read on the hand after drawing three rounds of trumps. Put yourself in the south position and try to find the correct line of play.

Since you know that west has four-one in spades and hearts, you should fear the possibility of diamonds not splitting. You probably notice that west appears to be having trouble discarding as you draw the third trump from east. So you should play one more trump (leaving one more trump in your hand) to see what west discards.

You must try to picture west's hand. Note that if diamonds are splitting (three-two), then you will simply have twelve tricks off the top. But if west has four diamonds, you can still make the hand on a strip-squeeze-end-play, which is a thing of beauty.

If west discards a third spade, picture him with one spade, four diamonds and three clubs. Cross to the queen of diamonds in dummy, ruff a spade which reduces west to diamonds and clubs, and then play ace, king and another diamond. West is now in and must lead clubs. Since east opened the bidding, you play east for the king – play a low club from dummy. Thus you score two club tricks and make your slam.

If west had kept two spades, then you would have seen the eight or nine of clubs discarded. You have nothing to lose by playing the ace and another club. Lo and behold, the clubs tumble and your seven of clubs and little club are now two good tricks upon which you pitch your two little diamonds, getting to dummy with diamond queen.

Neat hand. If you found the correct play, then you should be considered an expert!

A-8 FIVE-CARD SUIT WEAK-TWO BID

IMPs (Swiss)	Neither Vulnerable
You Hold: ♠ x	
♥ AQ10xx	
♦ 10xx	
♣ 109xx	

What would you bid in first seat?

Many aggressive modern experts would open this hand 2H even though you hold a not-so-good five card suit. It is possible that you will get doubled and go for a minus 800 or 1100 or worse because you preempted 2H with this hand, but that is unlikely. Your side will more often gain the advantages wrought by preempting the opponents, aiding your constructive bidding and lead direction.

Many players, especially at IMPs, prefer to retain the old fashioned length requirements of seven cards in the suit for a three-level preempt and six cards for a weak-two bid. Even these somewhat conservative players sometimes make exceptions with extra high quality shorter suits. You would be unlikely to go for a number or be criticized for opening three clubs with AKQxxx or for opening two hearts with AKQJx.

The above hand is hardly a suit of great quality. Even if you had merely the nine in addition to the given hand, that is AQ109x, not many experts would find fault with the bid.

Notwithstanding all of the above, when I picked up this hand in the North American Swiss Teams Championship (New Orleans Fall Nationals in 2003), I chose to open 2H. Although I would have been happier if I had the nine of hearts as well; my choice of bids was strongly influenced by the fact that I had the ten-nine fourth side suit, the singleton spade, and even the ten-third of diamonds.

When you play poker, you occasionally take an aggressive action on a hand because you judge that the number of good things that can happen outweigh the bad. On this hand, I essentially gambled that the preemption, the constructive bidding aspect, and the lead direction, would be more valuable to our side than the risk of getting caught for a penalty. I was right.

My partner raised to 4H although we had less than twenty points between us. The vulnerable game would score up +420 with favorable splits or with less than perfect defense by the opponents. Our partner's at the other table defeated a spade partial.

For practice, try playing the hand with the king of spades lead. Note that on the actual lie of the cards, the game can be defeated with good defense if the West hand plays second-hand-high with the queen of diamonds.

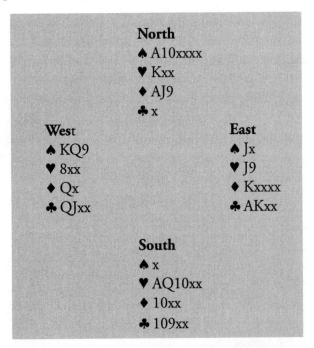

North
- ♠ A10xxxx
- ♥ Kxx
- ♦ AJ9
- ♣ x

West
- ♠ KQ9
- ♥ 8xx
- ♦ Qx
- ♣ QJxx

East
- ♠ Jx
- ♥ J9
- ♦ Kxxxx
- ♣ AKxx

South
- ♠ x
- ♥ AQ10xx
- ♦ 10xx
- ♣ 109xx

SECTION A

One of the main advantages of aggressive weak two-bid hands like this, where your partner has a good fit with you, is that the bidding might go 2H, pass, 4H, and all pass. Quite often, even if you can't make your game, the opponents might have had the opportunity for a game but never got into the bidding.

A-9 THE FIVE-CARD SUIT PREEMPT

MATCHPOINTS	Not Vulnerable vs. Vulnerable
You Hold: ♠ xxx	
♥ xx	
♦ xxx	
♣ AKJ9x	
The Bidding: P P ??	

What call would you make in third seat?

Here is another match point special. Your partner is a passed hand and you are not vulnerable against vulnerable. Since you certainly do not have enough to open, even in third seat, you could pass. Or you could essentially psyche a one club opening bid – call it an ultra light opening bid, but then you would probably have to pass any bid your partner makes.

But wait! There is another, even better possibility. Simply open the hand with a 3C preempt! It is true that you don't have seven clubs or even six clubs, but what are a few clubs among friends? You have made the all important lead director, and since your partner is a passed hand and knows you have a weak hand, whatever he does should work out well.

If partner has a fit and raises you, so much the better. You might even be close to making something. If he bids a suit of his own, then at least you have a few trumps for him and the ace-king of clubs. Preempting with a very strong five-card-suit is actually a very high percentage action, especially at match points.

The only weakness or disadvantage of the bid is that occasionally you might get doubled and go for a large number – which is certainly an acceptable risk at matchpoints. The better your suit, the less likely you are to get doubled. What is the minimum strength of the five-card suit to keep it a high percentage action? A good rule-of-thumb is that you should always have at least three of the top four honors.

One nice aspect of this somewhat offbeat five-card suit preempt is that it is equally effective against all levels of players. Some ultra-aggressive bids are recommended mainly against good players and not against weaker players on the theory that you don't need a sledge hammer to crush a peanut. However, the above five-card-suit 3C preempt is recommended against all opponents, especially at match points. Weak players can find even more ways to get in trouble at higher levels.

Perhaps you have wondered that if preempting on a five-card suit is a sound action, what about preempting on a four-card suit? In third seat favorable vulnerability, is it reasonable to preempt with AKQJ or perhaps AKQ10? Yes – but that is more than aggressive. You will find this discussed in Section F.

A-10 OVERBID? DON'T KEEP THE SPADE SUIT A SECRET

IMPs	Both Vulnerable [Vanderbilt]
You Hold:	♠ K10xxx
	♥ --
	♦ xxx
	♣ Kxxxx
The Bidding: 1C	2H ??

What call would you make with this hand?

If you merely bid 3C, showing good club support with six to nine high-card points, it is a good thing that you are reading this book. Whereas this hand argumentatively fits that description of 3C, this hand is actually much too strong for a mere club raise – because of the void in hearts, the five-card side suit (spades) and the fifth trump (if clubs are trumps). If you did choose to bid 3C on this hand, it should have been because you decided to *walk* the hand, a tactic discussed in the next section, which, by-the-way, would probably be ineffective on this hand.

When I picked up this hand in a Vanderbilt KO match, I thought that the aggressive 2S bid was obvious, even though I had only six high-card points and a two-level new suit bid normally shows ten point or more. One major (pun intended) reason to show your spades is because spades are higher than hearts. Clubs aren't.

A good poker player when faced with a choice of reasonable actions, often tries to anticipate how the subsequent betting is likely to proceed. My left hand opponent bid 4H, which was certainly not unexpected, and my partner bid 4S with his three aces including the ace-third of spades, ♠Axx ♥Axx ♦xx ♣AJxxx. Although we had only nineteen points between us, spades split three-two and I claimed ten tricks after playing a few cards. As you can see, the opponents had a cheap save in 5H.

At the other table, a world-class player holding my cards cue bid 3H to show his club fit first, and perhaps create an illusion of strength. He probably planned to come back in over the almost-likely 4H with 4S. Can you foresee a possible problem with this approach?

My partner's hand at the other table, over 4H, quite reasonably bid 5C on his three aces, five-clubs and knowledge that partner's hand rated to be short in hearts. But 5C had three inescapable losers and went down one.

If you are going to make an aggressive bid, make the bid that rates to do your side the most good. If you are fortunate enough to have the spade suit, don't keep it a secret unless you find yourself in highly unusual circumstances, such as in B-9.

A-11 NO NEED TO SHOW SECOND SUIT

MATCHPOINTS	Not Vulnerable vs. Vulnerable [BW 499]
You Hold: ♠ x ♥ QJ10xxxx ♦ Kxx ♣ xx	
The Bidding: 1S 3D 4C ??	

What call do you make with this hand?

Here is another favorable vulnerability (white vs. red) special where anything goes. The opponents may well be able to make a grand or small slam – if they can get there. You mission, should you choose to accept it, is to get in their faces.

There may be something to be said for bidding some number of hearts. Perhaps if you look around the table and see one or more novices, you might try to get fancy and confuse everybody, including your partner. If you are playing against average or better players, I would not recommend dragging out your hearts suit because it might help the opponents in their bidding and also if they aredeclaring the hand.

Using principles stated in the first several hands in this section, your main objective at this juncture is to jam up the lines of communication as efficiently as possible and as safely as possible. You would like to shut out all lower level descriptive bids and, of course, you would also like to shut out Blackwood.

A simple 5D bid here does mostly everything. They can no longer bid Blackwood and five-level bids are ambiguous. It is true that if they double you, your side will probably go for a telephone number, but since you have almost zero defense, they can probably make a much bigger number in slam.

SECTION A

Another simple virtue of the 5D bid is that it doesn't force them to bid slam. If either of the opponents bid 5S, they may well play it there, probably making overtrick(s) unless your partner turns up with several tricks.

Note that a 6D bid would be even more destructive when considering bidding space; it also shuts out 5N and bids through 6C. But 6D has the drawback that if they do bid, they will probably bid a slam that they can make. If they merely double you, you might even go for more than the amount of their slam. For example, down six is minus 1400, whereas 6C making is 1370.

A-12 BID GAMES AGGRESSIVELY

IMPs	Both Vulnerable
You Hold:	♠ AK98xxx
	♥ x
	♦ AQxx
	♣ x
The Bidding: P	1D ??

What call would you make with this hand?

Although some players would prefer to merely bid 1S with this hand, because of the 1D opening in front of me, I decided to gamble out 4S. Since my partner was a passed hand, slam was very unlikely, and I would like to prevent them from finding a possible fit in my two short suits. I evaluated that I needed only one good card from partner to make a vulnerable game, which might have been too little for him to bid with. No one doubled.

Perhaps the main danger with making an aggressive bid with length in the opener's suit is that the chances of getting doubled are somewhat increased – in this hand I had four diamonds. Since I have length in diamonds, my left hand opponent (LHO) is more likely to be short in diamonds and may have more of my suit. Clearly LHO would love to double 4S with queen-jack fourth or queen-ten fourth, since his partner opened the bidding.

The good news is that since my partner is also likely to be short in diamonds, and more likely to have some spades, the diamonds will be ruff-right for me. When ruffing a suit, it is obviously much better to have an opponent who is also short in the suit being ruffed, to be sitting in front of your hand that is ruffing instead of over ruffing you.

As I had hoped, left hand opponent (LHO) led his partner's suit, the nine of diamonds. The dummy was basically cardless for me, but it did have the seven doubleton of spades and a doubleton diamond.

The play of the hand was interesting (see the next page).

As I won the king of diamonds with my ace, I played out the hand mentally. If the spades split two-two, I could make the hand unless my LHO had two honors. If he had two honors and ruffed the third diamond in front of the board, then he could get back to his partner in either minor and ruff the fourth diamond high for the setting trick.

Instead of playing queen and then another round of diamonds, I tried to muddy-up-the-waters and break communications by playing my singleton club toward the queen-jack. It worked. They won the club and played ace and another heart.

The Hands:

North
- ♠ 9x
- ♥ Jxx
- ♦ xx
- ♣ QJxxxx

West
- ♠ QJ
- ♥ Kxxxx
- ♦ 9x
- ♣ Kxxx

East
- ♠ 10x
- ♥ AQxx
- ♦ KJ10xx
- ♣ Ax

South
- ♠ AK98xxx
- ♥ x
- ♦ AQxx
- ♣ x

Now I played queen of diamonds, then another diamond toward the board. LHO ruffed in but could not get back to partner. I ruffed his return, drew one trump, successfully ruffed my last heart on the board, then ruffed back to my hand to draw the last trump. I made the vulnerable game. We needed it to win the Swiss match by 4 IMPs.

At the other table, my hand overcalled with one-spade. After a negative double and a 2H bid, it tried 2S, and sold out to 3H, making 3. Faint heart seldom wins fair maiden.

A-13 WHEN IN DOUBT, BID CLOSE VULNERABLE GAME

IMPs	Both Vulnerable [ACBL 103]
You Hold:	♠ 98xxxxx
	♥ Qx
	♦ x
	♣ Qxx
The Bidding:	1D X 1H ?

Sixty-five percent of the expert panel chose to bid 3S with this hand which is generally the book bid with a long suit, weak hand. But this time, you have seven instead of the usual six, a singleton in the opponent's suit, and two queens on the outside, in suits that your partner supposedly supports, via his take out double. Not only that, but you are vulnerable at IMPs, wherein the scoring favors bidding close vulnerable games. For example, if the game is on a finesse, you gain 10 IMPs if it's on, and lose only six IMPs if it's off.

Bidding 4S can win even if 4S goes down. Every good poker player knows that when he makes a big bet, there are two ways it can win. He can win if he has the best hand, but he can also win if the opponent goes wrong – that is, the opponent does not call the bet with the better hand. So if you make the two-way 4S bid, it might make; and even if it would not make, the opponents might bid five of a red suit, which might go down. Your two outside queens might well add to the defense by supporting your partner's cards.

Note what might happen if you bid only 3S. First, you might miss a lucky game that they bid at the other table. Secondly, suppose the opener bids a game (3N or 4H), which gets passed around to you. Do you really want to defend? Or would you take what now rates to be a save in 4S? Close decision and either could be wrong. If you save, you probably will get doubled – which on this auction is more likely to go down and now the opponents know it.

When in doubt in these situations, it is usually correct to bid the two way close games and let the opponents have the decision problems. Good poker players strongly prefer to be the aggressive bettors and let the opponents decide whether or not it is right to make the dubious call.

Cross reference: see also D-15 for another slam level application of this principle.

A-14 AGGRESSIVENESS OR SANITY ?

IMPs	Both Vulnerable [BW 1198]		
You Hold:	♠ AQ10xx		
	♥ KJx		
	♦ A10		
	♣ Kxx		
The Bidding:	1S	2S*	X	3H
	P	P	3S	P
	??			
* A Michaels Cue Bid			

What call would you make with this hand?

There are some hands where you have very accurate knowledge of the distribution and there are warning signs that suggest that the aggressive contract actually seems like the less dangerous contract. This sometimes occurs when you choose an aggressive 3N contract in lieu of a three-level partial because you suspect that bad-splits or defensive ruffs are looming.

When this hand was rated by an expert panel, sixteen chose 3N and eleven chose to pass. I would bid 3N, more out of fright than aggressiveness. Why? Let's review what we know about the distribution.

Partner's double is penalty oriented and says that he has at least ten points and he probably wants to double at least one of the opponents suits. Thus, he usually denies a spade fit. With three or more spades and ten or more points, partner would routinely cue bid 3H – the opponent's known suit. Your right hand opponent's 3H bid probably shows three or four hearts; otherwise he might have bid 2N to inquire about his partner's minor suit. If this is the case, your partner probably has one or two hearts – which is consistent with his not doubling 3H.

Since your partner competed to 3S, which is not forcing, it seems clear that he has only ten or eleven points with two spades; probably a doubleton honor since he is bidding at the three level. Since partner has four or three major suit cards, he has nine or ten cards in the minor suits. If he had had a six card (or longer) suit, he probably would have bid three-of-a-minor. Partner probably has five-four or five-five in the minor suits

We also know that left hand opponent probably has five-five in hearts and one of the minors. If he has one spade, then spades are splitting five-one. If he has two spades, he will probably lead his singleton, which could cause you trouble if you play in 3S.

If you bid 3N however, you will probably get a heart lead which might give a trick that you would not get in 3S, if LHO has AQ fifth of hearts.

The above hand seems like *déjà vous* to me; several years ago I held a somewhat similar hand in the exact same bidding situation. In that hand, I also held fourteen points with the ace-king fifth of spades, king-jack doubleton of hearts, and king third and ten third in the minors. I bid 3N on that hand because I feared playing in 3S. It turned out very well because I made 3N with a heart lead after allowing LHO to cash his hearts and squeeze his partner.

Since it worked in that hand where I only had a doubleton heart, 3N is probably right in this hand for many of the same reasons. I might even have the heart suit stopped twice. I think that the panel chose correctly.

One thing for sure in a hand like this – don't expect for anything good to happen if you play it in spades. There will be bad splits in every suit.

A-15 HIGHLY SPECULATIVE GAME BIDDING

IMPs	Vulnerable vs. Not Vulnerable [BW 104]
You Hold:	♠ KQx
	♥ xx
	♦ AKJ9xx
	♣ xx
The Bidding:	3H P P ??

What call do you make in balancing seat?

When this hand was presented to a *Bridge World* panel of experts, thirteen panelists voted for the double, but ten panelists voted for the highly speculative 3N without any stopper!

In order to understand why many experts chose this highly speculative 3N, you must first realize that the preemptor's partner probably does not have good heart support since he would probably raise liberally – especially at this vulnerability. If you add up your points (thirteen) and the points probably held by the preemptor (probably 5-9), then the other two players together will hold about half the deck.

Thus, since your partner will hold ten points or more about half of the time, 3N will make, by hook or by crook, almost half of the time.

Be aware that if you double (balancing take-out double), there are many hands that will have good plays for 3N where your partner will chose to bid a black suit – and a 4-3 spade game might have several trump losers.

The take-out double might seem like a more conservative action and will probably have less large undoubled negative scores, for example, 3N down five undoubled. Nevertheless, the double could easily lead to a doubled suit contract disaster.

Perhaps the bottom line on bidding a gambling 3N with this sort of hand depends mainly on more general gambling factors such as how much you can afford to lose or if you are in a situation where you must take a chance to win. In bridge, the state of the match or how one team compares to the other team are often key considerations.

A-16 TWO-WAY SLAM ACTIONS

IMPs	Vulnerable vs. Non-Vulnerable [BW 104]		
You Hold: ♠ AQ9xxx ♥ -- ♦ QJxxx ♣ Q10			
The Bidding: 2H	3C	4N	??

What call do you make?

Fifteen members of the expert panel who astutely suspected that the 4N bidder was fooling around, or as we say when we do it, "trying to create an illusion of strength," voted for the double. But what do you say with a double besides the assertion that you have some cards? How will your double help your partner make decisions?

One thing we know for sure is that the 4N bidder is prepared to play in 5H doubled. Doubling 4N might suggest that you are interested in doubling 5H. What are you planning to do over 5H? Which black suit will you bid?

I strongly agree with the five members of the panel who voted for the 5H cue bid. What better response to an illusion of strength bid than with yet another. Just what does 5H show? First round control? That's what you have. Partner could have the right cards to make six or even seven.

But the main point here is that even if partner does not have the right hand, there is some chance that the opponents will come to your rescue. If the opponents are prepared to play 5H doubled, then they might well be interested in saving over a confidentially bid 6C or 6S slam.

We have here another action that can be right two ways. There is a fair chance you can make some higher level contract and there is also a fair chance that either opponent will save at 6H or higher. This is clearly better than playing 5H doubled, which probably would have been a good result for the opponents.

A-17 LIBERALIZED LEAPING MICHAELS

IMPs	Neither Vulnerable
You Hold:	♠ x
	♥ KQxxx
	♦ AJxxx
	♣ xx

What call do you make after a 2S opening weak-two bid on your right?

Soon after weak-two bids were popularized in the 1940s and 1950s, one of the standard defenses became what I have always called the western/two-suiter. If your opponent opens a weak-two bid in either major, an immediate cue bid of that suit (on the three level) asks partner to bid 3N with a stopper in that major. If the cue-bidder then bids a suit over partner's 3N bid, then the cue bidder has a strong two-suited hand. Many partnerships have various additional understanding as to which of the two suits is bid first and what is forcing, but the general idea is to provide a method of bidding a big two-suited hand, probably at least fifteen high card points or more.

Sometime in the 80s, a convention called Leaping Michaels became fashionable. Its name is perhaps a reflection of its similarity to the very popular Michaels Cue Bid, where an immediate cue bid after an opening bid shows a two-suited hand. In Leaping Michaels, if an opponent opens with a weak two bid in either major, then a jump to four of either minor shows a two-suited hand (at least five-five) with that minor and the other major. Perhaps the main advantage of Leaping Michaels is that partner immediately knows which two suits you have.

Most partnerships play that Leaping Michaels shows a good hand – again, probably at least fifteen points. What do you bid with the above hand? Pass? 3H or 3D?

In keeping with the modern trend of getting into the auction aggressively, in July, 1988, I wrote a *Bridge World* article entitled "Liberalized Leaping Michaels" in which I recommended liberalizing the point count requirements for a Leaping Michaels bid. With the above hand, I recommend bidding 4D, which shows at least five-five in diamonds and hearts (the other major) and no specific point count requirement but "with sanity prevailing."

Since Leaping Michaels takes you to the four-level, sanity requires having at least nine or ten points in the long suits as the rock-bottom minimum for the bid, perhaps slightly less white versus red.

A-18 AN OLD CONTROVERSY RESOLVED

MATCHPOINTS	Both Vulnerable [ACBL 403]
You Hold: ♠ x ♥ Q10x ♦ AJ9x ♣ KQ10xx	

What would you bid in first seat?

There has been a long standing controversy as to whether it is better to open 1C or 1D on five clubs and four diamonds. In short, those who favor 1D profess that by opening 1D and then rebidding 2C, you have bid both of your suits. Those who favor opening with 1C fear that opening 1D and rebidding 2C distorts your hand and might get partner to correct to diamonds when the hand belongs in clubs.

Note that if you open 1C and partner bids one of a major, you are not allowed to bid 1N (holding a singleton) or 2D (reverse showing seventeen or more points). So what would you open with the above hand?

It is my opinion that the answer lies in your partnership's approach to basic bridge competition. Since more than half the hands you play are part score hands, as opposed to game hands and slam hands, it is very important to orient your bidding to compete aggressively. A good general rule-of-thumb when the points are equally divided is that you want to compete and push the opponents to the three level. In these situations, once the opponents have reached the three-level, you peacefully defend, unless you have two or more points in distribution, a singleton for example.

If your partnership is dedicated to the proposition that you will normally take risks in order to push the opponents to the three level, then it is slightly better to open the above hand with 1C.

When you have nine cards in the minors, your opponents are likely to have an eight card or better major fit. Perhaps the most typical scenario favors opening one club. You open the above hand with one of a minor. Your left hand opponent doubles or bids a major. If the points are equally divided, then your partner has between six to ten points and will often make a one level bid (including 1N). Your right hand opponent will often bid two of a major (has a fit with partner), it is then your bid.

In this very frequent scenario, if you had opened with one diamond, bidding 3C would risk partner correcting to 3D. If you had opened 1C, you would be able to bid an aggressive 3C (which could be a six-card or longer suit and might push the opponents to the three level) rather than sell out to two-of-a-major. There are numerous situations in poker where you choose between close alternatives because you foresee being able to compete more effectively later.

A-19 AGGRESSIVENESS OVER TWO-OF-A-MAJOR

IMPS	Vulnerable vs. Not Vulnerable [1972 World Olympiad]
You Hold:	♠Kxx ♥A ♦AQ10xx ♣J9xx
The Bidding:	1S P 2S ??

What call would you make with this hand?

Playing match points, there would be no problem with this hand. As mentioned in the previous hand, at match points you do not let the opponents play their two-of-a-major fit if you have any reasonable alternative. At match points, you would bid 3D with this hand and perhaps try to push them to 3S.

But at IMPs, especially in the finals of the World Championship (1972, Italy vs. United States), would you come in red versus white with this hand? If there are four diamonds on your left, you might get doubled and go for a big number when the opponents don't even have a game! Team captain wouldn't like that.

But even at IMPs, you have to contest the part scores and be competitive. Otherwise the opposition will "six IMP you to death" – a typical part-score swing is five or six IMPs. Although you know that you could easily go for 800 on this hand, do the opponents know it? It is rare to double the opponents into game at IMPs without a very strong holding. And in this hand, it is unlikely that the opening bidder will have enough to double 3D with a known spade fit.

So would you risk a bid? What is correct with this hand?

Back in 1972, Benito Garozzo, chose to bid 3D with this hand. Fortunately for him, he found his partner with a four-card fit and a stiff spade. His partner bid 5D which made! Plus 600 for Italy.

A very good United States player at the other table chose to pass on this same auction, so they peacefully defended 2S which made. These results do not prove that it is correct to be aggressive. But in view of the big picture, where the opponents must keep in mind the possibility that you could have an eight or nine card suit, it seems right to test your poker luck here.

SECTION B
CONSERVATIVENESS

INTRODUCTION – GO SLOWLY

Although many of the more exciting moments in bridge are wrought by super aggressive bidding leading to big gains, there is another side to that coin. Often times the *bid 'em up* aggressive bids fail miserably for big losses. In both bridge and poker, it is essential to understand that bravado is not always rewarded. It is often better to proceed with caution, slowly and deliberately – close to the vest. And sometimes, a slow trap is the best option.

One of the most important concepts in poker is that money not lost, spends just as well as money won. If you want to increase your net winnings, you must also try to conserve your losses. Before you drive fast, you should master driving slow. How does one acquire the wisdom to know when to hold 'em and when to fold 'em?

A good poker player will often evaluate a given situation and realize that although he could win the pot if he were lucky, the chances of his winning are not sufficient to justify further investment. Prudence dictates that he should fold up his tent and withdraw as cheaply as possible. A more flamboyant and aggressive player may pursue and achieve the victory against the odds, but in the long run, that victory may cost many times what it won.

In bridge, there are often telltale circumstances that indicate danger or at the least, awkwardness in communications. Certain hands sometimes stand out and smack you with negative signs. You can often win on these hands by losing less. And again, although some more flamboyant and aggressive players may bid on and make the 25% game or slam, in the long run, they will not beat the odds.

Sometimes at bridge, as in poker, it is best to go slowly and try to trap – especially against overly aggressive opponents. Opponents who have been successfully trapped, often give you further opportunities. Carefully consider all the odds; your opponent might get lucky and you might end up trapping yourself.

In the following hands, there are some ominous situations which suggest a lighter touch. When going around curves, a heavy foot on the gas pedal sometimes results in a crash. Instead of a bid 'em up attack, sometimes you should just back off and let it go.

It is sometimes possible to adopt a wait-and-see approach, or perhaps transfer the decision(s) around and get help from your partner and/or the opponents (discussed in Section C).

B-1 DON'T MAKE ANTI-PERCENTAGE PREEMPTS

MATCHPOINTS	Both Vulnerable [ACBL 403]
You Hold: ♠ Q9xxx ♥ x ♦ xxx ♣ QJxx	
The Bidding: P P ??	

Would you open a weak-two spade bid on this hand?

Most average players would look at this hand and wonder what the problem is. You might think that the hand is an obvious pass, but aggressive matchpoint players tend to loosen up a bit when they are in third seat and not vulnerable. I once opened this exact hand with a weak 2S.

The reason I am starting this chapter with this hand is because this is the hand I played when partnered by the late great Oswald Jacoby, which I referred to in the Introduction. After my 2S opening, my left hand opponent overcalled 2N and his partner raised to 3N. Ozzie dutifully led from his doubleton spade, which together with my 2S bid picked off the queen of spades – declarer would have had a two-way guess.

Had I passed instead of opening 2S, the bidding would have gone 1N – pass –3N and then Ozzie would have made his normal "fourth from his longest and strongest" lead from king fifth of clubs, which would have held the hand to three for a decent score instead of a bad score for letting them make five.

Ozzie was very nice about it and understood that I was trying to make life difficult for the opponents. He also pointed out to me that all preemptive bids are a gamble and that sometimes the gamble loses, for example, when they double you and you go for a big number. Normal preempts are a good gamble because they have a lot of advantages when weighed against their disadvantages.

One of the bigger advantages of a preempt is that it usually gets your partner off to the right lead. Ozzie said that he didn't object to my having only five spades, but that opening queen empty fifth is a dubious lead director. If you lose the percentage advantage normally gained from lead directing, then perhaps the overall percentages of success of the preempt are lowered to where it becomes a losing action. If I had opened QJ10xx or even QJ9xx, there would have been a much greater likelihood that that suit was the best lead.

To make his point clearer, Ozzie asked me if I would invest money in certain poker hands. The hands he gave were clearly below average hands and no good poker player would voluntarily play them. I got the point. Although it is often sound bridge to preempt the opponents, I believe Ozzie was right about this hand. Don't be aggressive if it goes against the odds.

B-2 DON'T PUSH TO LOW PERCENTAGE GAMES

MATCHPOINTS	Both Vulnerable [ACBL 302]
You Hold: ♠ xxx ♥ Axx ♦ Qxxx ♣ AQx	
The Bidding: 1C 2S ??	

What call do you make with this hand?

Here is another hand where, if playing with an old Roth-Stone player (very sound opening bids), you might bid 3S, probably fetching a 3N bid from your partner if he has a spade stopper.

But playing modern day duplicate bridge, it is quite possible, and perhaps even likely, that your partner has opened up a typical twelve or thirteen point hand, perhaps even a "good" eleven. Bidding 3S could easily end up in a match point disaster with your side going minus two or three hundred.

When this hand was presented to an expert panel, the majority of the panel chose to make the off shape (but heavy in high card points) negative double. Assuming that the opponents remain silent, you will probably pass whatever suit your partner bids, although if partner bids 2N, showing extra values after your negative double, you would happily raise to 3N.

Note well that you are essentially going quietly rather than aggressively putting all of your eggs in the basket where your partner has you covered – he happens to have a good hand. Note also that if partner did have enough to actually make a game opposite your square hand (at least a good fourteen points with a five card or longer club suit), then he might have chosen to open a tactical 1N. If he has a big distributional hand, he will probably make a forward going bid. You will not miss game frequently because of your underbidding.

B-3 HELP PARTNER STAY LOW

MATCHPOINTS	Neither Vulnerable [ACBL 302]
You Hold: ♠ KQx ♥ Jxxx ♦ xxx ♣ xxx	
The Bidding: 1H 2H* ??	
*Michael Cue Bid (shows two suits, spades and a minor)	

What call do you make with this hand?

Here is another application of the principle: conserve your losses before they start. Unless your partner is a very sound opening bidder, you should tread very cautiously with this hand. Because your opponent, who bid Michaels showing five spades and five card minor, probably has five spades, your partner might well have two or less spades. Thus your hand may be worth very little to partner, and trumps might split badly. It is quite unlikely that your side has a game; and it is quite likely that you will get overboard if you bid freely.

Even though you have four trump and six-points, which would normally be a mandatory raise, it is much better in this situation to simply pass and then compete if they try to stop below 3H. Even though you have four trumps, you have no ruffing values on offense, so you would rather defend three spades as your side might well take five tricks. Looking at your hand, you are much more likely to take five tricks on defense than nine tricks on offense.

If your partner has enough to make a game in hearts opposite your hand, he may well bid again. If you bid 3H, partner would certainly carry on to game with something like ♠xx ♥AKQxx ♦KQJ ♣QJx (eighteen high card points) which has four losers off the top.

There are many times in bridge when you have to make a judgment based on all the data and knowledge that you currently have. On this hand, because your king and queen of spades has so much greater defensive value than offensive value, you clearly choose defense.

B-4 WHEN IN DOUBT - DON'T DOUBLE

MATCHPOINTS	Both Non-Vulnerable		
You Hold: ♠ x ♥ Q87xx ♦ xx ♣ AKQxx			
The Bidding: 1S	1N	X	P
P	2H	X	3D
P	P	??	

What call do you make with this hand?

This is a hand that I would normally open with. My partner opened the bidding in first seat and then passed my double of 1N. I have a singleton in my partner's suit. All good reasons to double, and I am still licking my chops after getting to double 2H! Now that they have run to 3D, am I really supposed to double 3D on two small? Note that partner didn't double 3D. From this I conclude that they have a 9 or 10 card fit. Should I just hold my breath and double on high-card points?

Let's say that I decide against doubling 3D. Should I bid 4C? Would that not be forcing? Even if 4C was not forcing (I think it is), would I expect to make 4C? Probably not. There was a strong 1N bid at the table, and I also know that the heart suit is splitting badly. What would you do?

If you decide to double 3D, you are worse off that me. My LHO has 6 diamonds (a 6-3 fit) and even though they only have seventeen points between them, it's cold for three. My partner's king and another diamond are in front of the ace-queen.

My partner chose to lead his stiff 10H (not unreasonable) and it made four. Declarer's only card was the king and another heart. It was a trouble hand for our direction, and we scored above average for avoiding big trouble.

It often pays to simply go quietly.

B-5 PUSH OR WAIT

MATCHPOINT	Neither Vulnerable [BW 720]
You Hold: ♠ Ax	
♥ J10xxx	
♦ Kxx	
♣ Qxx	
The Bidding: P 1D 3C ??	

Here is a hand where you could bid 3H which would show at least ten points and at least five hearts – which is essentially what you have, but your queen-third of clubs is a questionable value, and you certainly don't want to play game opposite a minimum or even a flat-medium opening bid.

The big problem with 3H is that it is forcing, and partner will be forced to bid even with minimum or medium (around fourteen points) opening bids which will probably get your side too high. Since you have ten points and the 3C bidder will normally have six to nine points, your partner will have eleven to fourteen points about two-thirds of the time that he holds eleven or more points.

Also, as in an earlier hand, when partner opens one-of-a-minor, it is less likely that he holds a fifteen to seventeen point hand since he did not open 1N. In many aggressive match point partnerships, your partner would also be unlikely to hold a good fourteen point hand, on which he might also stretch a tactical 1N not-vulnerable.

A good poker player would have no trouble with this hand if he knew that he was roughly a two-to-one favorite to go minus if he bid 3H forcing. By simply passing, you are a big favorite to go plus. If your partner reopens showing extra values or at least the right shape, then you can take your best shot. A good poker player would not want to voluntarily put himself in a losing situation.

So this is also a hand to go quietly – at least for the moment.

B-6 RISKY BUSINESS

IMPs	Vulnerable vs. Not Vulnerable
You Hold:	♠ xx
	♥ Jxx
	♦ A10x
	♣ AQ10xx
The Bidding: 1D	3H ??

What call do you make over the 3H preempt?

There you are, vulnerable at IMPs with a hand that you would normally open with, albeit a very minimum opening bid. You partner has opened the bidding, and now the nasty opponent has stuck it to you with a 3H preempt. What are your options?

You could bid 4C, but that is forcing and it is not clear that you want to get that high, especially if partner has a minimum. You could make a negative double, planning to bid 4C (a nonforcing bid) if partner bids 3S. If partner bids 4S, you would then have to bid 5C! That could turn into a nightmare.

You could make a highly speculative 3N bid, but that could be quite embarrassing if they run the first seven heart tricks against you. Nevertheless, if I decided that I had to bid something rather than pass with this hand, I would shoot out 3N.

You could pass. You certainly rate to beat 3H. Note that if partner has a good hand he will not pass, and if he does not pass, whatever he does, you will certainly spring back to life. The main danger in passing is that your partner might have a medium hand with no good bid that is cold for game (probably 3N).

The expert panel was rather divided on this hand. Seven voted for the pass. Five voted for the negative double. Four voted for the speculative 3N. Three voted to bid 4C and one person voted for 4D.

I like the conservative pass on this hand because I believe that there are far fewer hands where we will miss game if I pass than hands where I will get us too high by making a bid. A good poker player often settles for a sure plus rather than risk disaster by trying to accomplish too much.

B-7 DON'T GET DAZZLED BY GREAT TRUMPS

MATCHPOINTS	Not Vulnerable vs. Vulnerable [BW 1198]
You Hold: ♠ Axx ♥ AQxxxxx ♦ 10 ♣ xx	
The Bidding: P 1H 4D ??	

What bid would you make?

When this hand was presented to an expert panel, sixteen chose to bid 5D, three bid 4N, and nine chose the safe 4H. It seems that there is a tendency to over-evaluate hands with a great trump fit.

Although you certainly have excellent trump support for partner, you nevertheless, have only one outside honor. Give your partner a typical hand with the king-fifth of hearts and most nine or ten outside points (especially without the king of spades), and you might well go down in five. If partner happened to have a wasted diamond honor, you could even go down in four! It seems likely that if partner has a minimum opening bid, he is much more likely to make four than six.

The only minimum hands where partner is cold for a slam are ace-king-queen-jack of clubs or ace of clubs with king-queen-jack fourth of spades, but partner might not bid a slam with thirteen points and no singletons.

Your chances of reaching a good slam would be better if there was a slam try available which described your hand. A 5H bid would probably ask partner for a diamond control. The 5D bid is somewhat ambiguous. If partner happens to hold most of the missing cards, he might assume you have first round control of diamonds or more high-card values. Bidding 4N Blackwood is also inappropriate; even if partner has all the aces, he might have no play for slam.

Although I tend to take an optimistic (aggressive) view in most bidding situations, I believe that any move toward slam here is both risky at the five-level and does not really describe your hand. The bottom line is that partner is more likely to hold a hand that will end up going down than a hand that will make a slam.

Finally, note that because of the vulnerability, if you bid a bad slam there is little chance that the opponents will save you by sacrificing. If the vulnerability were reversed (you vulnerable, they not), there would be more to be said for bidding an aggressive slam which might stampede the opponents into a save.

I would bid the conservative 4H.

B-8 DON'T GET DAZZLED WITH SOME EXTRA

IMPs	Both Vulnerable [BW 400]		
You Hold:	♠ AKJxx		
	♥ AK		
	♦ Jxx		
	♣ J10x		
The Bidding:	1H	P	1S	P
	2D	P	3C	P
	3H	P	??	

What would you bid with this hand?

When this hand was presented to an expert bidding panel, fifteen panelists chose to bid 5H and ten chose 4H.

What do we know about partner's hand? Does he have six hearts? Not necessarily. He would bid 3H whenever he had nothing else to bid. He does not have three spades. He does not have five diamonds. He might have something like ♠xx ♥QJxxx ♦AKQx ♣xx or even one spade and three little clubs. He made no effort to show more than a minimum.

If he does have six hearts, he might have something like ♠x ♥QJxxxx ♦AKxx ♣Qx.

Perhaps the main problem with the panel's 5H bid is that it is somewhat ambiguous. Is partner looking for something specific? Or is it merely quantitative? What should partner do over 5H with ♠x ♥Qxxxxx ♦AQxx ♣Ax? Note that 6H would be on a 3-2 trump split if either hand held the ten of diamonds, but partner would probably not bid the slam on his minimum and poor trumps.

It would be quite aggressive to bid 5H over the non-forcing 3H bid, especially if you do not play fourth suit forcing to game (probably more than half the world), then. Although partner will probably have at least some play for 5H even when he has a minimum, it is not clear that he will bid and make a slam more often than he will go down in five.

All in all, I would characterize 5H as a bid that I would make if I had a reason to gamble, for example, if I felt I was behind in an IMP match.

B-9 HANG 'EM HIGH

MATCHPOINTS	Neither Vulnerable
You Hold: ♠ Kxx	
♥ Qxxx	
♦ Q10x	
♣ Kxx	
The Bidding: 2S P P 3C	
P ??	

What call do you make with this hand?

Note first and foremost that you are playing matchpoints. If you were vulnerable at IMPs, this hand would have a different answer. At matchpoints, your partner is going to strain to balance over 2S.

You do not get rich at matchpoints defending two-of-a-major. Partner would probably balance with a sub-minimum hand and a decent club suit. He might go down in 3C even with your fine dummy. He would rather go down one or two (not vulnerable), than have the opponents make 110 or more.

It is true that your partner might have a fifteen point hand or even more and not have adequate distribution (short hearts) for a double. But more often he will not have enough to bid or make a game. If you happen to bid 3S, and if he happened to have a sound opening bid or better, and if he also held the queen and one spade and bid 3N and got a spade lead, you might make it.

Since partner is bidding in the balancing seat, he knows that you have some points. In fact, he may be bidding partially to protect your hand. With some fifteen or more point hands and a spade stopper, he might have gambled out 3N.

The bottom line here is that your bid is much more likely to lead to a minus score than a successful game. So give partner some room here. He might need it.

If your partner does hang you with a hand like this, it has recently become fashionable to accuse him of *Clinting* you (from Clint Eastwood movies).

B-10 TAP THE BREAKS

MATCHPOINTS	Not Vulnerable
You Hold: ♠ 10xxx	
♥ Axx	
♦ Qx	
♣ Kxxx	
The Bidding: 1D P 1S P	
4C* P ??	
* Splinter (singleton club, game-going hand)	

What do you bid with this hand?

There are some partnerships which require the automatic cue bidding of any first-round control between the splinter bid and four of the major. With that understanding (only), you would be required to bid 4H, that is, cue bid your ace of hearts on the way to 4S.

most partnerships do not have that understanding (the automatic cue bid). A splinter bid declares that there is game in the hand. If responder suspects that there might be a slam, he shows interest in further investigation by cue bidding.

In this given problem, the question is whether or not the hand has interest in slam. If you want to tell your partner that you have extra values and want to explore the possibility of slam, you would cue bid 4H (your ace). If you want to tell your partner that slam is unlikely, do not cue bid 4H. Instead, bypass 4H and sign off with 4S.

To evaluate the above hand for slam interest, note first that the king of clubs is a wasted (not working) card because the splinter bid showed a singleton or void club. Secondly, this hand has no trump honors! The burden of the trump suit is entirely on your partner, and since you probably have a four-four fit, even the jack of spades may be important.

If partner does not have the ace of clubs, then you would not want to play slam unless partner has the ace, king and queen of clubs, even then you might go down on a four-one split.

To make slam likely, partner would need at least something like ♠AKQx ♥Kxx ♦AKxxx, nineteen specific points. But if you bid 4H, showing ace of hearts and slam interest, your partner will probably bid Blackwood with a hand such as ♠Axxx ♥KQx ♦AKJxx ♣x, which has no play for even five spades.

B-11 TREE DOWN ON THE HIGH ROAD

MATCHPOINTS	Neither Vulnerable [BW 900]
You Hold: ♠ Ax ♥ A108xxx ♦ Ax ♣ Kxx	
The Bidding: 1C 1H P 1S 2C ??	

What call would you make with this hand?

When this hand was presented to an expert panel. Nine chose to double, which is probably a penalty double, eight chose the conservative 2H and six chose to cue bid 3C, which is probably better than 2N.

The problem with this hand is that you will probably need a major suit fit in order to make a game. In hands where there is an opening bidder who rebids his suit, and hence usually has entries, you will probably not make 3N unless you have extra values – points or tricks.

Assuming right hand opponent has a good six card or longer suit, you do not rate to get rich by doubling 2C unless your partner has a good hand, in which case you might make more by bidding a game. If you cue bid 3C, your partner might have to rebid 3S on a five-card suit and a minimum hand.

Perhaps the bottom line on this hand is that if you bid 2H, and partner is not good enough to bid again (for example, raise to 3H), there are very few hands where you will miss a game. If there is no game in the hand, 2H is probably a fine part score contract.

When playing poker, there are many times that you perceive a certain danger, and you proceed cautiously. In this hand, when the opening bidder rebids his suit, it usually means that 3N is going to be harder to make. Thus, you can afford to be just a bit more conservative.

Perhaps the general helpful hint for today is in a close situation; you stretch to bid a game if there are favorable signs or if something good has happened. The other side of the coin is that you don't stretch to bid close games when there are danger signs or if you can foresee a problem ahead.

B-12 GIVE PARTNER SOME ROOM?

IMPs	Both Vulnerable [BW 499]		
You Hold:	♠ xxx		
	♥ Q10x		
	♦ Kxx		
	♣ Axxx		
The Bidding:	1D	2S	P	P
	X	P	??	

What call do you make with this hand?

When this hand was presented to an expert panel, fourteen experts chose the 3S cue bid (game going), twelve chose 3D and six chose 3C.

Many of the 3S bidders made the aggressive overbid because they were vulnerable at IMPs, where making a vulnerable game has a large pay off. Others mentioned that their partners were not likely to compete with balanced minimums when vulnerable.

Although both of those reasons are true, partner is never anxious to pass out two-of-a-major, especially when you might have a penalty pass. Partner is going to strain to find a bid over 2S, and will frequently double with a minimum hand and relatively short spades. Partner will usually double with many medium hands that will not make a game opposite your hand.

For example, your partner would certainly reopen with a double with ♠x ♥Axxx ♦AQJx ♣Qxxx or with ♠Kx ♥KJxx ♦AQJxx ♣xx. Both of those hands will end up going minus if you bid 3S. Partner might well compete with even lesser hands. Of course, if partner has a very big hand and he knows from the auction that you probably have some points, he will often bid 3N over your three-of-a-minor bid.

I would take the low road on this flat nine-point hand and bid either 3D or 3C if we frequently play Equal Level Conversion. Equal Level Conversion would be employed with the second example hand in the preceding paragraph, where the 2-4-5-2 shaped reopening double is planning to correct a 3C bid to 3D. Equal Level Conversion does not promise extra values – merely four cards in the other major.

B-13 GO QUIETLY? NOT CLEAR

MATCHPOINTS	Neither Vulnerable [BW1000]
You Hold: ♠ AKxx ♥ QJ9xx ♦ KJ10 ♣ A	
The Bidding: 1H 3D P P ??	

What call do you make with this hand?

Here is a hand where I was on the fence – but you should draw your own conclusions. Actually, I wasn't in doubt about bidding, I was on-the-fence about whether to put this hand in the Aggressive Section or, in deference to the expert panel, here in the Go Slowly Section – sometimes known as the Coward's Section, though we all know that coward's live longer.

Twenty-six of thirty-four experts on the *Bridge World's* panel chose to pass and take the likely plus at match points. I do not agree. I would simply bid 3N on the theory that we might belong there. Surely most of the other match point players will not pass 3D with my hand. What if my partner was making a slightly conservative pass of 3D?

The consensus of comments by the expert panel reflected that partner might be broke and that 3N could easily go for a number. This is correct, but my right hand opponent (RHO) does not know what I have and will probably not double. One amusing possibility if my partner is broke with a long spade suit, is that 3N down two not vulnerable is a good save against 3D making.

I do not fully understand the panel's mass conservatism. If I have eighteen high-card point, and we assume the left hand opponent has about eight points for his preempt, that leaves fourteen points remaining for the other two hands. Partner will frequently have about half of those fourteen points. That might well be enough for game in no-trump. It is perfectly standard to overcall a three-level opening preempt with a sixteen point strong no-trump hand.

The biggest danger to 3N is if LHO has the ace-queen long in diamonds and chooses to under lead, and RHO has two or more diamonds and an entry. If RHO has a singleton or void diamond, I really like my chances in 3N. Since partner did not bid 3H, my partner is slightly more likely to have more of the missing diamonds than my RHO. My partner might also have found a bid with a short diamond.

I went along with caution on the preceding five hands, on this hand I draw the line and go for it. Is it true that cowards live longer than heroes?

B-14 SLOW PLAY - WALKING THE DOG

MATCHPOINTS	Both Vulnerable [Lancaster, Pennsylvania Regional, 1998]
You Hold: ♠ AKxxxxxxx ♥ xx ♦ x ♣ x	
Bidding: 1N ??	

What do you do with this freak hand?

Every poker player knows that there are some hands where you go slowly not because you don't know what to do, but because you want to act like you don't know what to do. You try to convince the opponents that you are fishing in on a not-so-good hand by simply checking, calling or by making very small bets. Especially at no-limit poker, you slow-play a good hand and try to lure the aggressive opponents into your trap.

Every poker expert also knows that when you slow play any big hand that is not an immortal lock (a hand that can't possibly be beat), there will be times when your slow-playing allows an extremely fortunate player to end up with a hand even better than yours. Call it an occupational hazard.

Included in the annals of Going Slowly with bridge bidding are a number of distributional trapping hands. Instead of trying to jam or preempt the opponents, you simply bid the hand slowly and allow them plenty of room to communicate that they have the bulk of strength in the hand. You continue to bid on, perhaps over their game, on a level which would normally be much too high – perhaps a sacrifice bid on your part. They double you as they should in due course, but because of your freaky distribution, you can make your doubled contract.

In the above hand, one possibility would be to preempt, 4S, and hope your partner has a trick for you. Perhaps a better approach (look around the table) is to simply bid 2S and walk the dog. When I held this much-discussed hand, I was playing the Cappelletti Over No Trump convention (of course), so I bid 2C to show a one-suited hand. I intended to bid the cheapest number of spades whenever it was my turn, but the left hand opponent bid 3N which was passed around to me!

I really wasn't sure that I wanted to defend! The 1N bidder might have had a spade stopper or my partner might have a trick and I might make 4S, but I passed and led the ace of spades. Everybody followed!

I ran nine tricks for a score of plus 500. That scored ten out of twelve match points. Two other dogwalkers got doubled in 3S and were plus 730. This was not a good hand for the strategy of leading fourth from your longest and strongest.

B-15 SLOW PLAY - WALK THE DOG

IMPs	Both Vulnerable			
You Hold:	♠ --			
	♥ xx			
	♦ J10xxx			
	♣ A109xxx			
The Bidding:	1C	1D	1H	??

What call do you make with this hand?

When this hand was presented to an expert panel, twenty-five out of thirty-three chose to bid 5D, which is certainly a reasonable bid. But, unlike a number of the aggressive hands in Section A, this hand is not about shutting out the opponents. Indeed, this is a very sophisticated hand and with appropriate handling, it might produce a big win. I think this hand is too good to bid 5D.

The best way of describing this hand is to compare it to picking up four-of-a-kind at poker. Although you possibly could be beat, you are certainly willing to take your chances and not try to narrow the field as usual. Instead you want to encourage as much contribution into the pot which will soon be yours.

You have to understand the situation before you can reach that conclusion. On the given auction, the spade suit, your void, has not been bid. Someone has to have a five-card spade suit.

If your right hand opponent (RHO) has the five spades, then he also has six or more hearts, since with five-five he would normally respond 1S. If your partner has the five spades, then he has six diamonds. And if your left hand opponent (LHO) has the five spades, he has at least five clubs. Many players open 1C with five-five in the black suits.

It is most likely that the spades are divided five-four-four. Your partner is highly likely to have some wasted values in spades, but it is quite unlikely that your partner has more than one club. If your partner does have more than one club, then LHO would be likely to have four hearts, and your partner would probably have a singleton heart. The bottom line is that you are highly likely to make 5D – almost as likely as four-of-a-kind will win at poker.

Since the opponents have already found hearts, and since your partner probably has defense against spades, you do not want to stampede your LHO into bidding 5H over your 5D bid, a very likely possibility. Rather you would like to bid 5D as if you are saving, since most opponents tend to believe that the five level belongs to the opponents. You should simply go slowly, walk the dog, and bid 2D. You will surely get to bid again.

B-16 THESE BOOTS WERE MADE FOR WALKIN'

MATCHPOINTS	Neither Vulnerable [BW1000]
You Hold: ♠ Q8xxx ♥ Q9xxxx ♦ x ♣ x	
Bidding: 1C X P ??	

What call do you make with this hand?

You are playing poker and you have two choices as to how to proceed with a big hand. One of the choices tends to describe your hand quite accurately; the other choice, tends to hide a major aspect of your hand. Which do you choose?

You are playing bridge and your partner makes a take-out-double of a minor suit, usually asking for the majors. You are looking at a weak hand but with six-five in the majors. No one is vulnerable. How do you proceed?

There may be something to be said for cue bidding 2C on this hand to allow your partner, the take-out-doubler, to pick his best major. But of course this also tells the opponents that you have support for both majors.

To a poker player, this hand plays itself. Slow play the hand, starting with 1H. I would not bid the spade suit unless partner gave some indication that he didn't have hearts. For example, if partner bids diamonds, it shows a one-suiter in diamonds and tends to negate his support for the majors. If partner does bid diamonds, I would bid spades, which might be our best fit.

If partner does nothing to negate his take-out double, I believe it is poor tactics to ever show the spade suit. It might help the opponents take the save or help them defend. Walking the hand in hearts might well lead to our getting doubled for a good score, because the opponents will know that they have the majority of high-card points.

A number of the expert panelists who also bid 1H on this hand, mentioned how they would be bidding spades later. They would benefit from poker experience. Assuming that your partner has at least three hearts for his take-out double, there is really no reason to show the spade suit. Since you are walking the hand, your partner has no need to know.

SECTION C
NEED INFORMATION

INTRODUCTION - GET HELP

When playing poker, there are usually good reasons to play both fast and aggressive or slow and passive. Many poker hands contain conflicting factors and ambiguous signs. Deciding how to proceed is often difficult.

At bridge, it is often correct to take a fast aggressive approach, but at other times, as we saw in the last chapter, it is best to go slowly, listen, and try to avoid disasters.

Bridge bidding has evolved into a complex science, and often, your partnership has developed special bids and conventional understandings to help in problem situations. In poker problem situations, every good poker player has his own little bag of tricks and techniques.

There are times when none of your bidding conventions apply and you simply do not know which way to proceed with a hand. At such times, you must try to stay flexible and direct the bidding such that you can gain useful information from your partner or from your opponents.

In the following hands, you will experience bidding situations where special partnership understandings will help you find out what you need to know, though there are other situations where you can only guess and play percentages. There are many situations where partner's slightest input (sometimes even his pass) will tilt the odds affecting your decision. And, as every good poker player knows, there are times when you also gain valuable information from your opponents.

Otherwise put, suppose you were walking somewhere and you came to a fork in the road without road signs. Would you simply guess which direction to go? Or would you guess to take the road which appeared to be more frequently traveled? Or, rather than risk going in the wrong direction, would you stop and wait for someone to come by who might furnish information?

C-1 GET HELP - ELEVEN!

MATCHPOINTS	Both Vulnerable [circa 1995]
You Hold: ♠ AKJxxxxxxxx ♥ x ♦ x ♣ -- (eleven spades)	
The Bidding: 1H ??	

What call would you make with this hand?

Playing poker, you often pick up a great hand in an early seat and you are not quite sure how to proceed. If no one has a good hand, you do not want to bet too much and scare everybody out. If the other players do have good hands, you would rather they open the betting so that you might judge how much to raise. If you check and everybody checks around, that is a disaster. In these situations, it is often best to start off with a minimum bet and see what develops.

One of the greatest get -help hands I have ever held was also the only eleven-card suit I have ever held. Obviously, I am cold for eleven tricks, and the only question is whether partner has any red aces. A 4N bid at this point would be unusual for the minors, usually showing 6-6 in the minors. If I start off with a double, then my partner might think that a subsequent 4N bid was key-card Blackwood, the king of trumps is treated like an ace, in whatever suit he bids.

I quickly dismissed my thoughts of bidding 4S and allowing myself to be pushed to five. I would probably be preempting myself more than the opponents. It was my turn to bid and I had to do something. Thus, I made the poker *get help* bid – a simple 1S. *Cross Reference: see also F-11.*

It worked out even better than my expectations. My left hand opponent (LHO) bid 2S, a cue bid in support of hearts. My partner who was void in spades passed. My right hand opponent bid 3C! That was music to me ears, since my partner (my wife) and I had recently started playing exclusion Blackwood.

I jumped to 5C, *exclusion Blackwood*. This unusual jump to the five level asks my partner to show aces excluding the ace of clubs. Wasn't this just perfect!

My partner, looking at the ace of diamonds, obediently bid 5H, showing one ace. RHO doubled 5H. I bid 6S, and to make it even sweeter, LHO doubled 6S!

There are many occasions in bridge where it is unclear as to which road to take. But when you are looking at a hand where you can bid solo to a high level all by yourself, it is sometimes better to listen than to leap.

C-2 GET HELP - SEVEN-SIX

IMPs	Both Vulnerable
You Hold: ♠ --	
♥ --	
♦ AKQxxx	
♣ AJxxxxx	

What do you open in first seat?

Yes, you have picked up a super-freak. How do you get to the right spot? Note that there are no known scientific methods/ conventions – like Blackwood – available to find out what you really need to know. Even if you happen to have *asking bids* available, usually after 2C openers and specific jumps which tend to elevate auction, to find out about club honors, what happens when partner shows no honors?

What would you open? And what is your game plan?

There is actually a simple approach which will yield reasonably good results. In standard bridge, when you hold a distributional two-suiter, you normally open your longest suit and then rebid your shorter suit an appropriate number of times. For example, if you held a good hand with five hearts and six diamonds, you would normally open 1D and then rebid hearts twice if it is practical. Partner would then know you have at least five hearts and longer diamonds.

In the above hand, you might plan to show partner your 7-6 pattern by opening 1C and then rebidding diamonds three times, if possible. But that sequence would not necessarily get you to the right contract.

Note that although you have longer clubs, you have better diamonds. If partner has two card support for each of your suits, a fairly likely possibility, you would prefer to have diamonds as your trump suit. Why? Because if you are playing in diamonds and the clubs split 3-1 (slightly more likely than 2-2), you might be able to ruff the third round of clubs, especially if dummy happens to have the jack or ten of diamonds.

The bottom line on this hand is that if partner has equal length in the minors, you would prefer to play the hand in diamonds. It just so happens that in standard, if you open the hand in diamonds and then later make a big jump in clubs, your partner with equal length will usually preference you back to your first suit. Note that if your partner happens to have equal length but has a club honor and chooses to leave you in clubs, that is fine also.

So the recommended bidding on this hand is 1D, to be followed by a 6C bid (!) unless your partner makes a very unusual bid in the majors.

C-3 HIGH LEVEL HELP

MATCHPOINTS	Vulnerable vs. Not Vulnerable [ACBL 403]		
You Hold: ♠ Kxx ♥ AQ9xxx ♦ AQx ♣ J			
The Bidding: 1S	2C	2H	5C
P	P	??	

What call do you make with this hand?

"Help!" Let's face it. They got you! Now you have to do the best that you can. What makes sense here? You could try to guess how many spades to bid. Six?

Instead of guessing at 6S, perhaps the best bid here is 5N! When this hand was submitted to an expert panel, eight chose 5N, four chose 6C, three chose 5S and two chose double. Thus, twelve out of seventeen judged to bid a slam with this hand. But note that no one bid 6S, though all twelve probably expect to play in 6S.

Since partner passed the 5C bid around to you. probably a forcing pass, he is not interested in making a penalty double. You have more than enough to expect to make a high level contract. So what is the best call?

Since you are essentially interested in playing six or more of a major, you should bid either 5N or 6C to get partner's help as to which major. What do each of those two bids mean? Maybe some partnerships have discussed this type of situation, but most likely you haven't. In that case, both bids mean, "Help."

Is 5N the Grand Slam Force in the last bid suit? No, it is simply not. A jump to 5N might be the Grand Slam Force when there are other bids available, but over a five-level preemptive bid, 5N is often the only help-me-out bid available. Perhaps, 6C shows first (or second?) round control of clubs.

The 5N help-me-pick-a-slam bid has the extra advantage of allowing partner to bid 6C, which probably does show first round control of clubs? There may be a grand slam in these hands – but it will be your partner that has to bid it. You have already done everything you can do by bidding 5N. If partner does bid 6C, you would certainly bid 6D, and let him make the guess.

They officially got you with the 5C bid. So now you and your partner have to do the best you can and then guess.

C-4 GET HELP WITH DEFAULT BID

IMPs	Neither Vulnerable [BW 502]		
You Hold:	♠ AJ9xx		
	♥ xx		
	♦ AK10x		
	♣ Jx		
The Bidding:	1S	P	2C	P
	2D	P	2H	P
	??			

What would you bid with this hand?

In stark contrast to the previous exciting distributional hands is this perfectly mundane opening bid which has essentially run out of bids. Playing two over one forcing to game, you have shown your five card major and your four card minor. Your partner has just bid 2H which is natural, but might well be a convenience bid. He wants to hear more about your hand.

But you have absolutely nothing else to say – and you really have no exact way of saying that you have nothing to say. Certainly you can not pass in a game forcing auction.

If you rebid your spades, that would tend to show a not-so-good six card suit (since you chose to bid 2D instead of 2S) or a very good five card suit. If you rebid 3D, that would show a fifth diamond. If you bid 2N, having already shown five-four in the pointed suits, that would either show two-two with some sort of heart stopper or perhaps three hearts and one club. You have none of the above. Help!

So what do you bid? Although you would rather have three-card club support for a 3C bid, noting that you might have raised 2C to 3C immediately with three clubs, here you should simple bid 3C on your jack-doubleton. Note that the 3C convenience bid in a minor suit is certainly the least of evils in this hand.

When this problem was presented to an expert panel, thirteen chose the 3C bid and twelve chose to bid 2S. The main problem with bidding 2S is that your partner might play you for better spades (a major suit) and place the final contract in spades with two small spades – whereas, 3N or 5C might be better.

This problem brings up the interesting issue: What do you bid when you have nothing to say or no obvious bid? Is there a default bid? It is generally better to make a convenience bid in a minor. The default bid in hands where you can not pass is often the cheapest bid which distorts your hand the least. You can only hope that partner helps with his next bid.

C-5 GET HELP - FROM CAPPELLETTI

IMPs	Neither Vulnerable [BW 1200]
You Hold:	♠ AK10xxxx
	♥ AK10x
	♦ J
	♣ x
The Bidding: 1N ??*	
* You are playing Cappelletti/NT: 2C=(any)one suiter; 2D=majors; 2Major=that major and minor	

What would you bid playing Cappelletti over no trump?

There is definitely something to be said for the solo bid of 4S. Keep it simple. And indeed, the expert panel voted 15 for four spades whereas only eleven voted for 2D, which asks for a major. But is this a good gamble? Do you want to gamble if you don't have to?

Should we try to bring partner into the picture? The answer to that question is usually determined by just how descriptive your bidding will be in the given circumstances. In this situation, the 2D bid asking for a major will most likely fetch a 2H bid by your partner. Over 2H, you plan to bid a very descriptive 3S.

Note that if partner has four (or more) hearts and short spades, four hearts will probably make whereas four spades will probably go down. Note also that if partner has a gross misfit, you are one trick better off in spades (might even make). The two problems with going slow are that your partner might not bid a (lucky) game that happens to make, for example, two little spades, jack third of hearts and out. And the opponents might get into the auction and find a good contract.

Perhaps the crux of this particular hand and situation is whether we are more likely to get to the right spot with help from partner and possibly from the opponents, or if is it better to simply blast into four spades and hope something good happens. Although it is reasonably close, on this particular hand, I think the scale weighs slightly in favor of going slowly and getting help.

C-6 AN ILLUSION OF STRENGTH

IMPs	Vulnerable vs. Non Vulnerable [ACBL 903]
You Hold:	♠ 98xx ♥ x ♦ A ♣ AKQJxxx
The Bidding:	1C P P X ??

Ten out of fourteen experts voted to bid 3C. Some of them indicated that they would bid 3S over three-of-a-red-suit competition. Though you have eight tricks in hand, you are unlikely to have a game in view of your partner's pass – he is unlikely to have an ace or spades adequate to make a game with the take-out double behind him.

Since you certainly do not intend to have partner make any final decisions on this hand – in bridge, you often describe your hand to partner so that he can place contract – you have no reason to accurately describe your hand to partner, for example with a 3C bid, especially if you are also describing your hand to your opponents.

Is it likely to keep the opponents out if you bid 3C? Actually, you are rather likely to push them into a light game which they might make. Your left hand opponent might freely bid 3H and the doubler on your right might raise him to four on a good fourteen plus points with a stiff club. Then you certainly couldn't bid 4S red versus white!

This is the kind of hand where you want to keep the bidding low so that you know what to do, if indeed there is anything good to do. It probably won't hurt to give the opponents room, since your 3C barrage will be totally ineffective in keeping them out of the auction and might even push them into a light game that they can make.

Good poker players know that there are certain types of hands where you put your money in fast and there are other hands where you're best off keeping it low and watching what develops. This is clearly the type of hand where you want to encourage your partner, and the opponents, to help you decide what is best.

If you redouble, which supposedly states that you have a very strong hand, you cater to most of your needs. You will hear your left hand opponent bid a red suit and then you partner might do something. If he bids spades, you are certainly happy, whatever you decide to do. If he does something other than pass or bid spades, you might fly into three no trump, which even if it goes down, might be a good save. You might even make it – the best defense might be difficult to find.

C-7 BLACKWOOD?

IMPs	Vulnerable vs. Non Vulnerable [BW 302]		
You Hold:	♠ AKx		
	♥ AKQxx		
	♦ Ax		
	♣ J9x		
The Bidding:	P	P	3D	X
	4D	4S	P	??

What call would you make with this hand?

Here is a tricky situation where the nasty opponents have taken much of your badly needed bidding space. With a solid twenty-one points and a source of tricks, you are certainly required to make at least a try over your passed-hand partner's freely bid 4S.

Is this a hand where you should bid Blackwood? You could find out if he has the ace of clubs and the queen of spades (trumps). That might be enough to make a slam, and he should have more.

Partner might have enough for slam even without the ace of clubs. Almost any ten- point hand without diamond honors will have at least a play for slam. Since all you did was make a take out double of 3D, your passed-hand partner should have a good ten points or the equivalent to bid freely on the four level.

How can you get partner to help you out here? If you cue bid 5D, what will that say to partner? First, you are making a slam try, and second, he should notice that you did not bid Blackwood. Therefore you are not particularly looking for aces. Since he is a passed hand, he knows that you can not expect him to have more than ten points.

Since both opponents bid diamonds and you have the ace, partner is unlikely to have more than one diamond or a diamond honor. Therefore, if he has a hand with the queen or the queen-jack of spades, he is also rather likely to have two of the three missing club honors since all other honors are accounted for. But will he really bid a slam with just the queen of spades and the king and queen of clubs? Probably not.

The expert panel chose the 5D cue bid which might work – but might not. Partner might easily not bid the slam with makable values, such as ♠Qxxxx ♥xxx ♦x ♣Axxx or ♠Qxxxx ♥xxx ♦x ♣KQxx, or bid it on a going down holding (any good hand with bad trumps).

Once again, as in the previous hand, I think the concrete information obtained from Blackwood is most likely to lead to the best result. If partner has neither ace of clubs nor queen of spades, then stop. With one or both, go for it.

C-8 GET HELP - ACES

IMPs	Both Vulnerable [BW 303]
You Hold:	♠ AK10x
	♥ KQJ9xx
	♦ xx
	♣ A
The Bidding: 1H	3D 3N P
?	

What call would you make with this hand?

Your partner's 3N bid shows a willingness to play 3N opposite an opening bid. Because he was preempted, he could be stretching with as little as ten points, or he could have as much as fifteen or sixteen points. With seventeen points or more, opposite your opening bid, he might have made a slam try.

Looking at your fine trick-taking hand, there are many different hands your partner could have that would make a slam. You certainly have another bid coming! But how do you find out what you want to know? Note that a 4N bid here would be quantitative, not Blackwood.

An expert panel chose 5H as the best bid on this hand. Would you expect partner to carry you to six looking at two aces and the queen of spades? No way!

It is not possible for you to tell partner what you have, but you do have a way to find out if your partner has two key cards. If your partner has the two missing aces, then slam should be a very good bet. Thus bid 4C Gerber* if you play that.

If you do not play 4C Gerber in this situation, then I recommend the 4D cue bid, just to see what partner will do. If partner bids 4H, which shows secondary support such as a doubleton or an honor (ace), then you could bid 4N, which should be Blackwood if you had no way to ask for aces on your previous bid. But you would not be too unhappy if partner passed 4N with low slam interest, but he probably would not pass if he had two aces.

In poker, once you think you know something, you usually act on it. It is mainly when you are in doubt that you parry and seek more information. In bridge, when you think you know more about the hands than your partner knows, you should take control of the hand, rather than transfer the decision to your partner (like with a 5H bid here).

* Depends on partnership agreement re Gerber over no trump when 4N is quantitative

C-9 HELP PARTNER - IMPLIED CARDS

MATCHPOINTS	Neither Vulnerable [Regional Pairs]		
You Hold: ♠ xx ♥ Axx ♦ KQ10x ♣ QJxx			
The Bidding: P	P	P	1D
1S	P	2S	??

What call would you make with this hand?

Perhaps you should have passed this hand out in fourth seat, but now that you have chosen to open your twelve points, you simply can't give up without a fight. If the opponents play 2S, experience has taught that you will get a bad board if they make 2S unless they declare badly. If they go down in 2S, that would mean that your side could have made a part score.

Even though you merely have a minimum hand and your partner has passed twice when he might well have found a bid, you should not pass 2S here. Your partner, who must have some high-card points, may have an awkward hand and might not know what to bid. You are in good position to help out.

Let's review what we know about this hand. Both opponents are passed hands, which means that the 1S overcaller on your left probably has less than twelve points. The 2S raise on your right usually shows six to nine or perhaps even ten points. The opponents probably have a total of seventeen to twenty-one points between them. Since you have twelve points, your partner will have at least seven points (40-21-12) and perhaps more.

You know that your partner had enough points to respond, but he did not make a negative double which would have shown four or more hearts. And he did not bid 1N which would have shown six to ten points with a spade stopper. He probably has a hand with no good bid, such as three little spades, less than four hearts, less than four diamonds and about seven or eight points. It is very unlikely that he has a penalty pass in spades because of the raise.

Most average players with this hand would simply pass here on the theory that they have a rank minimum and they should not make another bid on the three level. Certainly, you can not make a reopening double here, since that would show extra values.

The winning action here is to anticipate partner's likely problem. You already know that he has something like ♠xxx ♥KJx ♦Jxx ♣Kxxx and will either pass 2S or bid 3D. He would be unlikely to bid his four-card club suit which is your best spot and might even make. Note that 2S is quite likely to make; if you play the hand and go down one or even two, that would be a better score.

Since your partnership is quite dedicated to the match point principle that you do not let the opponents play their two-of-a-major fits if there is any reasonable alternative, you should volunteer a 3C bid here – notwithstanding that you only have four-four distribution in the minors. It will make life much easier for partner as he will simply pass 3C or correct to 3D. Note that your 3C bid does not show extra strength, though you normally do have better distribution.

When you play limit poker, you frequently make value bets with hands that are not really strong enough to justify a bet. Because of various inferences about what the opponent(s) holds, you make the bet because it rates to be right.

SECTION C

C-10 HELP PREVENT THE PSYCHIC GRAB

IMPs	Neither Vulnerable [Regional Swiss]
You Hold: ♠ AJxx ♥ xxx ♦ Q10x ♣ Jxx	
The Bidding: 1D X 1S ??	

What call would you make with this hand?

Although it may look like a natural 1N bid because you have four spades and your partner made a take-out double, you must double 1S with this hand! Your partner made a take-out double which essentially asks you to bid a major if you have one. And you have one. Does your opponent really have spades?

Bid one-of-a-major over the opponent's take-out double when you have a weak hand and a fallback fit in the minor suit which your partner opened. Many games have been stolen with this psychic bid. The best way to help defend against it is to play a double of the one-of-a-major bid after your partner's take out double shows four or more spades with at least one honor and at least six high-card points in your hand.

When our teammate at the other table held this hand, she chose to bid 1N instead of the recommended double. Her partner raised to 2N and she chose to pass. The other hands were:

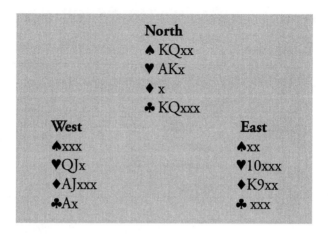

The opponent dutifully led a spade. When our teammate knocked out the ace of clubs, the opponent could see that his partner did not really have spades. He guessed correctly to shift to a low diamond, and they could have cashed five diamond tricks for down one, but they had a little accident and somehow blocked the diamond suit upon cashing the fourth diamond.

When we compared scores, our teammate was proud to have stopped short of game and to have made 2N. I would have bid 3N with eight points. Our opponents had bid the normal 4S against us which was cold for five!

Cross Reference: see F-6

C-11 TWO-SUITED CUE BIDS TO THE RESCUE

MATCHPOINTS	Both Vulnerable
You Hold: ♠ K10xx	
♥ x	
♦ AKJxxx	
♣ xx	
The Bidding: 1C P 1H ??	

What call would you make with this hand?

In most partnerships the choice would be between a take-out double and a 2D overcall. Both bids have problems since the opening bidder might well support hearts, perhaps at a higher level, and your partner, who passed over one club, might have some cards but might not have a bid. For example, if you double, partner might not have four spades but might have three diamonds; and if you overcall 2D, your partner will not bid on four spades.

If you happen to be playing Cappelletti Cue Bids you will soon get partner's help in choosing the appropriate contract.

Cappelleti Cue Bids apply when each of the opponents have bid a different suit, as in the auction above. Each of their suits becomes a cue bid, as opposed to a natural bid, as some people play. The lower cue bid, in this case 2C, shows the other two unbid suits but longer in the lower suit, in this case diamonds. The higher cue bid, in this case 2H, shows the other two suits but with longer in the higher suit, for example, five or six spades and four diamonds.

The Unusual 2N would show equal lengths – usually five-five – in the unbid suits, and a take-out double usually shows four-four in the unbid suits.

On the above hand, playing Cappelleti Cue bids, you would bid 2C, and then partner would have the best picture of your hand possible.

When this hand actually occurred, the opening bidder jumped to four hearts, and my partner, looking at the QJxx of spades took an excellent save in 4S, which was missed at the other table.

C-12 EQUAL LEVEL CONVERSION

IMPs	Neither Vulnerable
You Hold:	♠ xx
	♥ AQJx
	♦ AKxxx
	♣ xx
The Bidding: 1S	??

In the olden days of bridge, when you made a take-out double of the opponent's opening bid and then bid a new suit over your partner's response, that showed a very big hand. A very big hand was a hand too good to overcall, since overcalls are usually limited to about eighteen high card points.

In modern bridge, the above principle still holds in most situations but there is now one noteworthy exception called Equal Level Conversion. A take-out double at the one-level usually shows support for the other three suits; if responder to the take-out double bids the lowest of the three suits and then the take-out-doubler bids the next higher suit on the same level, it is called Equal Level Conversion and no longer shows a big hand. Instead, it merely denies adequate support for the lowest suit and asks responder to pass or correct.

The main reason why this change was made is clearly suggested by the above hand. The importance of finding a four-four major fit on competitive hands is clearly more important than showing a big hand – with which there are often jump or other big bids available.

Thus, the modern correct bid on the above hand is double. If partner bids clubs at the two or three level, you will bid 3D Equal Level Conversion, and partner now knows that you have five or more diamonds and four of the other major, here hearts.

You do not promise any club tolerance at all on this auction. You could even have a void.

C-13   A HELPFUL GADGET

IMPs	Neither Vulnerable
You Hold: ♠ x	
♥ xx	
♦ Kxxxx	
♣ Qxxxx	
The Bidding: 1N 2S ??	

If your partnership plays no conventions over this auction, you might stretch a competitive non-forcing 3D or 3C bid with this hand. One reason for bidding 3C is that if you get doubled, you can retreat to 3D.

Most partnerships that play the Lebensohl convention, where a 2N bid here would require the 1N opener to bid 3C, would probably bid 2N and then pass partner's forced 3C bid.

Note that both in standard and in regular Lebensohl, there is some amount of risk in bidding at the three level with this weak hand – compounded by the fact that you might pick the wrong minor.

There are some fortunate people who play Reverse Lebensohl where the 1N bidder bids his better minor over 2N. Thus, with that extra advantage, 2N becomes a very clear action indeed. Poker players would appreciate playing Reverse Lebensohl on this hand since we always prefer sure information to guess work.

For those interested, in Reverse Lebensohl over 2S, both 3C and 3H are competitive. To play 3D, bid 2N then correct 3C to 3D. A direct 3D bid over the 2H or 2S overcall is now free for another use, as you'll see in the next hand.

C-14 YOU ARE CORDIALLY INVITED

IMPs	Both Vulnerable [North American Swiss]
You Hold:	♠ xx
	♥ Kxxxx
	♦ xxx
	♣ AJx
The Bidding: 1N	2S ??

What call do you make with this hand? Would you like some help?

Most bridge partnerships will have mixed feelings about this hand. You have an eight point hand and a five-card heart suit, but which should you show? In standard bridge you can only show one. You can either make a competitive 3H bid, a 2N invite (if you are not playing Lebensohl, although nowadays, most serious partnerships play Lebensohl) or stretch a force to game.

Those fortunate people who play Reverse Lebensohl – invented by Kit Woolsey and myself – actually have a bid for this hand. A 3D bid directly over the two-of-a-major overcall shows a five-card or longer suit in the other major and invitational points. Knowing this, this opening 1N bidder can either play 3H from the strong side, or bid game in hearts or no trump.

If you look at the discussion of Reverse Lebensohl on the preceding page, you will see why the 3D bid is available for this purpose. Clearly it is advantageous to have these modern methods to help get you to the right contract.

C-15 HELP FROM JOE'S JACOBY

IMPs	Both Vulnerable [Regional Swiss]
You Hold:	♠ KQxx
	♥ x
	♦ KJx
	♣ Axxxx
The Bidding:	1S P 2N* P
	3C** P ??
* Jacoby 2N ** short club	

What call would you make and how would you proceed with this auction?

Having bid the Jacoby 2N, you know your partner has a singleton club. Although you have only thirteen points, if your partner has enough aces, you should have a pretty good play for slam. Should you bid your stiff heart or will partner think you are showing length?

You decide to bid 4C since you do have first round control. Partner bids 4D, probably the ace of diamonds. For lack of something better to do, you bid 4N, Roman Keycard Blackwood. Partner shows zero or three key cards, which must be three aces. You bid 5N and partner shows no kings.

Looking at just your hand, even if partner has only three aces and no other cards, your only loser might be the diamond finesse. But where are your winners? If partner ruffs several hearts in your hand, it is merely a matter of finding a twelfth trick in diamonds: five spades, two heart ruffs, aces hearts and clubs and ace-king diamonds equals eleven. You shoot out 6S. That is how the bidding went at the other table!

At our table, the bidding started out the same, but over 3C, my partner bid a 3S relay bid which forced me to bid 3N.

Then my partner bid 4H showing a short heart with at least ten working points. Since we both know about the short clubs and hearts, working points do not include the KQJ of hearts and clubs. Since we have at least a 5-4 trump fit we also exclude the jack of trumps from the working point count. Thus there are a total of twenty-seven working points in the deck (40-6-6-1).

To find out his exact working point count, I now used WorkWood, a 4N convention originally designed by the late Joe Goldberg (for more details see my *Bridge World* article, December '03). My partner responded 5H which showed thirteen working points. Eureka, I thought to myself.

I knew his entire hand, even down to the jack of diamonds. My hand was merely fourteen point, ♠Axxxx ♥Axx ♦AQxx ♣x, but he had the other thirteen, and I could count thirteen tricks by simply roughing two hearts in dummy!

I bid the twenty-seven working point grand and it made without any problems, as long as trumps do not split 4-0. Whereas the opponents at the other table felt they were shooting, or gambling, to bid the small slam and making seven, we bid the grand with confidence.

Isn't technology wonderful? Thanks for the help, Joe.

C-16 BERMUDA BIDDING CONTEST

MATCHPOINTS	Both Vulnerable [bidding contest]		
You Hold: ♠ AJxx			
♥ Qxxxxx			
♦ --			
♣ Axx			
Bidding #1: 1H	**P**	**2C**	**P**
3C	**P**	**3D**	**P**
3S	**P**	**4H**	**P**
??			
Bidding #2: 1H	**P**	**2C**	**P**
2S	**P**	**3C**	**P**
4C	**P**	**4H**	**P**
??			

What call would you make in each of the above auctions?

At the lavish Princess Hotel in Southampton, Bermuda, my wife Susan and I were invited to be contestants in a bidding contest which was part of the entertainment after the evening session. This was one of the five hands.

The contestant in Auction #1 was apparently confused and passed 4H.

The contestant in Auction #2 bid 6C and played it there.

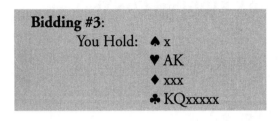

Bidding #3:

You Hold: ♠ x
♥ AK
♦ xxx
♣ KQxxxxx

The Bidding:	2D*	P	2N	P
	3C**	P	3D	P
	4C***	P	4N	P
	5H	P	??	

* Flannery 11-16 pts
** 4513 or 46 hand
*** 4603 distribution

Knowing that partner has 4603 distribution and two aces, what would you bid with this hand? Did our conventions really help out on this hand?

My partner bid 7C since it appeared that I had all of her losers covered. We received the full ten points for getting to the grand which the other three pairs missed, and went on to win the bidding contest by only one point more than Marty and EllaSue Chaitt.

** For extended Flannery responses see my article in *Bridge World*, March '03.

C-17 GET HELP DECLARER

IMPs	Neither Vulnerable [Monaco Bermuda Bowl 1976]

```
                        North
                        ♠ AK1094
                        ♥ Q82
                        ♦ Q2
                        ♣ 1062
        West                            East
        ♠ 85                            ♠ J732
        ♥ AK76                          ♥ 1054
        ♦ K10953                        ♦ 84
        ♣ J2                            ♣ K985
                        South
                        ♠ Q6
                        ♥ J93
                        ♦ AJ76
                        ♣ AQ74
```

The Bidding:	1D	P	1S	P
	1N	P	3N	P

How would you play 3N with these cards? Opening lead six of hearts.

Getting help from the opponents is certainly not limited to the bidding. Every good poker player knows that there are certain hands where it is unclear what to do and where it might be quite dangerous to make the first move, especially at no limit hold 'em. In these situations, it is often best to simply sit back and see what the opponents have in mind. Let them do their thing and see what develops.

In this classic hand, Paul Soloway won the opening lead with the jack of hearts and surveyed the situation. If he simply tried to cash spades and spades didn't split, he would be in big trouble since he also needed the spade suit for communication.

Since Paul did not want to break either of the minor suits, he employed the old theory that when you have nothing better to do, let the opponents help. So at trick two, Paul led a heart toward dummy! His left hand opponent (LHO) won his king of hearts and tried shifting to his 10 of diamonds. Paul hoisted the queen in dummy which held.

So there he was in dummy. What now? Paul played yet another heart and threw them in again! After cashing his last heart, LHO had to do something so he tried the jack of clubs. Paul was thus allowed to score his queen of clubs. Now that Paul had one heart, two diamonds and two clubs, he made the key play of a low spade to the ten, losing to the jack. Now Paul could claim nine tricks by overtaking the queen of spades. He wanted help – he got it.

SECTION D
LOOK AROUND THE TABLE

INTRODUCTION - PLAY YOUR OPPONENTS

Poker is a people game. One of the first things that every good poker player learns is that different people play differently. Although players tend to play similarly on good hands and bad hands, the greatest variance occurs in the play of medium or marginal hands. Aggressive players often bet marginal hands even more vigorously then their good hands. Tight and passive players often fold even the better marginal hands – so that they won't get tempted?

Bridge players are essentially the same. The aggressive players bid a lot, the sound players and the fearful players do not bid enough, and the medium players often do not make the most effective bid on their cards. Indeed, one reason why we have bridge bidding problems and expert panels to resolve them, is because bridge is a very complex game and the best bid on a given hand is not always clear.

The purpose of this chapter is to emphasize that the best bid on a given hand cannot be determined in a vacuum. Bridge is also a people game, at least to the extent that in most competitive auctions you really should look around the table. Every bridge expert knows that you must play your opponents.

Last but not least, somewhere in the equation you must factor in the impact of your own image. In poker, your image is a key consideration. When you take an action, what do people generally expect of you? Do you always or usually have what you should have? Are you known to be very aggressive? Or are you often random and all over the place? Different images contribute to the success/failure rate of your various actions, both in bridge and in poker.

If you have the reputation of being a sound expert who usually has his bids, then if and when you occasionally step out of line by making a somewhat loose bid) you are likely to get away unchallenged. If you have the reputation of being a loose wild man, your opponents will be out to get you. Just like in life.

In the following hands, when you try to decide what to do based on what you expect from the opponents, remember to also factor in what the opponents expect from you.

D-1 LOOK AROUND THE TABLE

IMPs	Vulnerable vs. Non Vulnerable
You Hold:	♠ --
	♥ --
	♣ --
	♣ AKQJ10xxxxxxxx
	(all thirteen clubs)

How would you open the bidding in first seat? There is no more appropriate way of starting off this chapter than with this classic bridge hand.

Although I have never held this hand or any other hand with more than eleven cards of the same suit – and I have held a lot of hands in my lifetime, thinking about holding this hand made a big impression on me when I was first studying the game of bridge.

If I remember correctly, it was Terence Reese, a British world class player and author, who analyzed this hand as follows: If you are playing this hand against expert players, open 5C. If you are playing against lesser players, open 4C. I completely agree and give due credit to a great expert and poker player, even if he never played poker. Perhaps this was the first look-around-the table hand that made me aware of the concept.

To state that you would like to play this hand in clubs would certainly be an understatement! Defending, obviously at the seven level, would be an IMP disaster even if the opponents go down several. It is hard to imagine but the other three players are all playing with a three-suit deck! And you only have ten high card points!

So how do you buy this hand in clubs? Obviously, you first look around the table. How aggressive or formidable are the opponents? Since all three other players at the table are void in clubs, no one wants to play in clubs, but if you start the bidding on the four or five level, the opponents bids will convey less information.

If it occurs to you to try a deceptive 2C opening bid to create an illusion of strength – don't! The opponents have at least one nine card fit, if not more, and you can be sure that they will both bid boldly, since they both have a useful void. It is quite likely that one or both would take the save against seven clubs if they thought you were bidding to make. Your goal is to make it seem like you are sacrificing against their slam.

Perhaps the most important lesson on a hand like this is do not walk (bid deceptively slow) the club suit and thus give the opponents enough room to exchange useful information. Against good players, it is safest to start at the five-level, thus shutting out all conventional ace-asking bids, but against very weak opponents, who might pass out 5C, perhaps you should start at 4C.

D-2 LOOK BEFORE LEAPING

MATCHPOINTS	Not Vulnerable vs. Vulnerable [ACBL 803]
You Hold: ♠ -- ♥ KQ109xx ♦ xxx ♣ KJ9x	
The Bidding: P P P ??	

What call would you make with this hand?

Should you open this hand in fourth seat? If so, what should you open? There are some old bridge theories about opening in fourth seat only when the sum of your high card points plus your spades exceed fourteen (Pearson Points).

A majority of the expert panel voted to open 2H. Many feared being outbid in spades though your partner might have a spade stack. Several experts voted to open 3H.

Usually the best solution to a highly distributional bridge problem is based upon looking around the table. You should especially look at the player in third seat who passed; he is highly likely to have at least ten points and four spades. Another factor is your partner's propensities in opening light eleven point hands.

Using logic similar to that of the Terence Reese bids given in the previous hand, I would suggest that if you decide to open this hand, the better your opponents, the more hearts you should bid.

If I was behind in an IMP match and thought I needed a big swing board, I might consider opening four hearts against very good opponents. That two-way action could easily work out well for our side. But, of course, it could also turn into a disaster.

The bottom line on a hand like this is heavily affected by the quality and type of your opponents. Look around before you act.

D-3 LOOK BEFORE DOUBLING

MATCHPOINTS	Both Vulnerable [ACBL 503]		
You Hold: ♠ KQx			
♥ xx			
♦ 10xxx			
♣ AQ9x			
The Bidding: 1C	1H	2H	3H
P	P	??	

A panel of experts almost unanimously chose to double with this hand. Most explanations were essentially, "Well, I have to do something!"

One lone dissenting opinion, it just happened to be my son, chose to pass because he already had showed a limit raise or better and his partner was apparently not interested in bidding further. Thus, game was unlikely and a protective double, a double to protect against the possibility that your side can make something, was unnecessary.

A good poker player, when in doubt as to what to do over an action by an opponent, usually takes a good look around the table to scope out his opponent(s). In this particular bridge scenario, a lot depends on how you judge your opponents. Are they frisky and apt to be bidding on scanty values? If so, there is much to be said for the risky double. I agree with my son that a double is very risky.* However, if you are playing against two rocks, a poker term for players who always have full values for their actions, or even against two solid-medium types who would not bid without cards or good shape, I believe the pass is best.

From a poker player's perspective, doubling in this type of situation is like calling a large bet with a mediocre hand, hoping that your opponent is bluffing. This a fast way to lose money if your instincts are wrong.

*Note that if the opponents hands were something like: ♠xx ♥xxxx ♦Qxxxxx ♣Kx opposite ♠Axxx ♥AQxxx ♦x ♣xxx (they have only fifteen points between them); they would always make three doubled and actually make four with most leads.

D-4 LOOK FIRST AND THEN GUESS

IMPs	Vulnerable vs. Non Vulnerable [ACBL 103]
You Hold:	♠ xx ♥ Jxx ♦ A10x ♣ AQ10xx
The Bidding:	1D 3H ??

What call would you make with this hand?

This is an extremely tough problem for bridge players because the most normal bid, 4C, might be both too high and forcing. The discreet, or cowardly, pass received the most votes, seven, from the expert panel; double (penalties) was a close second with five votes.

Admittedly, peacefully defending 3H could be the least of evils – anything is possible. Nevertheless, my opinion is that because you are vulnerable at IMPs and because you have two tens and a good five card suit to go with your eleven points, a pass is generally too wimpy, except against the most rock-solid opponents.

A good poker player would look around the table long and hard before folding his good hand (passing in bridge is often like folding in poker) to the 3H bet. If the player making the 3H bid seems to be the type who might be rather aggressive, especially when white versus red, I would consider it mandatory to bid.

If I felt that I had to bid, I would try 3N and hope partner has a heart honor. I once made a 3N bid on jack third in a very similar situation and caught my partner with a void! I lucked out when left hand opponent led the nine from nine-eight-small, dummy was void, and right hand opponent played his ten from ace king queen ten sixth to preserve communication, thinking that his partner surely had a doubleton since I bid 3N.

Occasionally, especially at matchpoint, when the preemptor is sitting to your left holding a long suit to the ace-queen, he will assume that you have the king for your 3N bid, and not lead the suit. He might lead an unbid suit hoping to find (an entry) his partner.

D-5 LOOK ACROSS THE TABLE

IMPs	Neither Vulnerable [WBL 102]		
You Hold:	♠ AKJxx		
	♥ Kxxx		
	♦ Ax		
	♣ Ax		
The Bidding:	2H	X	3H	3S
	P	4H	P	4S
	P	??		

What call would you make with this hand?

When this hand was presented to our expert bidding panel, shortly after 9/11/01, I did not foresee that two years later I would be writing a book section entitled Look Around The Table. Nevertheless, perhaps reflecting the sobriety and caution of those days, I submitted the following response:

Cappelletti: Pass – This problem must be answered in terms of your partner's inclinations. With most aggressive partners who would stretch to compete with heart shortness, I pass because there is more chance of going down in five than making six. And I already have showed a good hand and he does not have a maximum. But with a very solid partner, I would bid four no trump and bid slam if he showed a void.

Otherwise put, as several other panelists noted, your partner made a free bid (3S), and we could argue that he has to have something – say at least five or six points and some shape. But, then again, especially if he is generally very competitive, he might have less arguing that he was just competing or setting up the save with his singleton or void in hearts. Partner could also have as much as ♠Qxxxx ♥x ♦Qxxxx ♣KQ and slam would also go down.

However, if you think your partner would bid 3S only with sound values and that he might then bid only 4S with Q fourth of spades, stiff heart and KQ third or longer of either minor, then you would have excellent play for slam.

While we are fantasizing, if partner had as little as ♠xxxxx ♥-- ♦KQxxx ♣xxx, then you have excellent play for a grand slam! But, of course, he should not bid only 4S with that hand.

In situations where some minimums are good and some maximums are bad, as in the above examples, how can we get partner to evaluate what is good and what is bad? The simple answer is that in this hand, we can't. It is generally a bad gamble to risk going down in five if there is substantial doubt both that slam will make and also whether partner will bid six if it does make.

In poker we like to avoid actions where there are a number of ways to lose, and only one way to win. Much of this depends upon your opponent.

D-6 CAN THIS BE FOR REAL?

IMPs	Vulnerable vs. Not Vulnerable			
You Hold:	♠ --			
	♥ AKQ10xx			
	♦ AQJxx			
	♣ Ax			
The Bidding:	P	2C	2H	2S
	P	??		

What call would you make with this hand?

This looked like a dream hand at first, but suddenly it has turned into a nightmare! There comes a time in everyone's bridge life when you simply can't believe what seems to be happening! You are playing with bidding boxes, and sure enough, there is a 2H bid lying on the table in front of your left hand opponent (LHO).

If ever there was a look-around-the-table hand, this is certainly the prime example! You should first try to look around the table without people knowing that you are looking around the table. It would really help if you could detect a sly/knowing smile to your left. Then take another official look when LHO knows you are looking at him. Any clues? In poker we call them tells.

Otherwise put, when you are given a bidding problem such as this, the solution is not really a bridge problem. It is a poker problem. Someone makes a large bet? Do you call or fold? Look at your cards, then look at your opponent!

When you first looked at this hand, you judged that your partner needed very little for you to make a slam; for example, the king fourth of diamonds would usually make a grand . If your left hand opponent (LHO) hardly seems like the type who

141

would psyche (bid a suit that he did not have), it means that there are five or six hearts sitting in back of you. If he really has a 2H bid, you might easily go down in game.

What if your LHO is known to be a used camel dealer* type? If he is making a psychic bid of the heart suit, you might be on for a grand slam if partner has the right card(s). So what do you do?

What do you do when you hold a reasonably good hand at poker and someone makes a very large bet?

You have to decide whether you have enough to win if your opponent really has what he is supposed to have, or what the typical player would have, for his bet. And then, you must factor in the possibilities that he is stretching his values (bidding light) or if he is on an outright bluff.

In this given bridge situation there is yet one further complicating little detail. Assuming that you want to play game in hearts, which is not clear, how would you do that? The first time that you bid hearts, partner will certainly think that you are cue bidding the opponent's suit. And note that if you jumped to 4H, in modern bridge, your partner would assume that you were showing a splinter in hearts in support of spades, the suit he just bid.

The answer with regards to playing the hand in hearts is that experienced partnerships have discussed this situation. If you bid 3H and then rebid 4H over your partner's next bid, that shows hearts! Whenever you enter the auction with an artificial bid, or double, and could have a big one-suited hand, and you subsequently cue bid the opponent's suit a second time, it is a real suit. Otherwise the opponent's could steal you blind.

You might end up playing 4H. It might make. Or it might make a grand! Unfortunately it seems like the opponents got the best of this auction! It happens.

* Having spent much time in Morocco, this reference is an "accepted" quip and not considered an affront to camel dealers.

D-7 THE "I'VE GOT YOU" DOUBLE

MATCHPOINTS	Neither Vulnerable [StrataFlighted Pairs]		
You Hold: ♠ xxx ♥ x ♦ Q10xx ♣ KJxxx			
The Bidding: 1S	P	1N	2C
X	P	P	??

Here is a delicate situation to say the least. The ethics of the situation might often be tainted if your partner thinks for a while before passing the double. If the 1N bidder on your right also thinks, you know you are in trouble.

When I played this hand in a regional open pairs, the little old lady on my left doubled with great conviction. My table presence told me that she really had the goods. In fact she did have the ace-queen-ten-nine of clubs. She certainly had her double.

In view of what I saw and felt, it seemed clear to run to 2D, although that could easily be going from the frying pan into the fire. I was quite relieved when 2D was passed out, undoubled. My partner, a client, probably should have run from the double, having three-four-four-two distribution. The opponents blew a trick on defense and only beat me one in 2D. In 2C doubled, the opponents had at least seven unblowable tricks. Had I stood proud and tall in the pocket in 2C doubled, I would have gone for 300 or 500.

This very classic look-around-the-table situation illustrates how the odds change when the type of person making an action tends to convey information about the strength of the action.

In the next hand, this same thought process can be applied to a confident 3N bid.

D-8 THE CONFIDENT 3N BID

MATCHPOINTS	Not Vulnerable vs. Vulnerable

You Hold: ♠ 109xxx
            ♥ Qxx
            ♦ xxx
            ♣ KQ	

The Bidding: 3D 3N ??	

What call would you make on this hand?

The lady in front of me bid 3N in such a manner that I knew she expected to make many no-trump with her hand. She held her hand and admired her hand like she was looking at gold. Although my 4D save might have been dubious in other circumstances, in this situation it was quite clear that we were not beating 3N.

So I bid 4D. The gentleman on my left immediately bid 4H, like he was planning on bidding 4H anyway. Then my partner, who is, in theory, barred from further action, bid 5D.

The lady on my right screamed double like she expected to beat it big time. She was smiling like she loved her hand. The guy on my left, shrugged his shoulders and passed the double. She led the king of spades.

My partner, who had ♠xx ♥-- ♦KJ10xxxx ♣Jxxx, managed to take eight tricks and held it in to –500. That turned out to be a top since the opponents were cold for 7H or 7N on the show-up heart finesse.

But again, quite often what might otherwise be a marginal action becomes a clear cut action because of who or what kind of player is involved.

D-9 WHO DOTH?

MATCHPOINTS	Neither Vulnerable
You Hold: ♠ AQxxxx	
♥ AKx	
♦ KJ	
♣ Ax	
The Bidding: P P 1S ??	

What call would you make on this hand?

This hand is definitely a look-around-the-table hand. What kind of person bid the 1S? Was it a little old lady? Was it some kid who is playing frequent psyches? Was it a guy with an accent and a little mustache? Or was it a shady looking used camel dealer?

Are your opponents playing four or five card majors? If they are playing four-card majors and your partner has a singleton, you probably will only have two trump losers.

If you are playing against a player whom you expect to have his bid, then you should simply make the penalty pass. You should be thankful that you have received ample warning about the bad spade split.

If you are playing against a known psycher or the used-cameldealer type, then you probably should double and subsequently consider bidding or inviting a no-trump game.

If your partner has as many as five points, you might well make 3N notwithstanding the bad spade split.

Hands like this are particularly troublesome in bridge (*see also hand D-6*) because they fit no preconceived mold. If you can be flexible, and evaluate the people involved accurately, you have a much better chance of taking advantage of the adversity.

D-10 TO PLUNGE OR NOT TO PLUNGE

IMPs	Not Vulnerable vs. Vulnerable [ACBL 0903]
You Hold:	♠ x ♥ xxx ♦ QJxxxxx ♣ xx
Bidding: 1S X 2N* ??	
* Limit raise or better (Jordan)	

What call would you make with this hand?

An expert bidding panel selected 5D as the best bid. My son, Mikey, and his wife Shannon, voting-as-one on said expert panel, chose to pass, planning to save in 5D if the opponents bid a game. Both 5D and pass are very reasonable actions, but a good poker player does not just look at his cards when he makes such decisions.

First, you should take a good look at your opponents. Are you playing against two hotshot kids who tend to bid a lot? Or are you playing against two little old ladies. There is much more to be said for bidding 5D against two experts, who might even bid a makable slam if given room, than to take the 5D plunge against two beginners, who might even miss bidding game. But note that in light of your partner's takeout double, an opposing slam is quite unlikely, so there is much less incentive to shut out Blackwood.

Against weaker players you might even consider making one of the following creative bids on the above hand:

Bid 3N – obviously planning to run to 4D if doubled. It would be most effective versus a weak or novice player and would probably not be effective against experts. It would be even more effective if you are a conservative player or a little old lady.

Bid 3S (cue bid) then pass partners response if not doubled. Run to diamonds only if doubled. It might wreak havoc against weak opponents.

Bid 3C or 4C might well make opponents misevaluate their hands. But that might cause partner, who is on lead vs. spades, to make a disastrous club lead

If you don't like any of these big action bids, there is much to be said for just sitting back and waiting to see if they bid a game; they might have only 23 or 24 high card points between them. If they do bid the game, then you should bid 5D, which will probably go down two or three tricks and should be a good save.

D-11 A MARTY OR A NORMAN

MATCHPOINTS	Neither Vulnerable [BW 900]
You Hold: ♠ QJx ♥ Axxx ♦ AQJ10x ♣ x	
The Bidding: 1D 3H X P ??	

Here is another bridge problem which can only be resolved using poker skills. Even the bidding panel essentially said just that. It all depends on what kind of player made the 3H bid and what you expect the 3H bidder to have. Depending on the solidity or looseness of that player, you have to make appropriate adjustments.

There is some amount of bridge luck involved. If your partner holds the king-queen of clubs and the king of spades or king of diamonds, then the opponents hold both black aces and may well score it up. Or the opponents might go down one or two when you are cold for a game, probably 3N . On the other hand if your partner has the black aces and the pointed kings are on side for you, you might collect 800.

By passing 3H doubled you might get a great score (300+) six times out of ten and a bad score four times out of ten – they make it or slight plus is bad score. This is all fine if you want to gamble, but there is something to be said for simply trying to make 3N. If you go down several, they might have made 3H.

One highly respected player said that he would bid 3N in the qualifying rounds and pass in the finals. In the qualifying rounds you are merely trying to insure average plus scores. In the finals, you try to hit home runs.

Other comments were if you look around and see that the 3H bidder was Marty Cohen, known far and wide for his aggressive preempts, you would pass the double. If the 3H bidder was the late Norman Kay, know as a very solid player, you should bid 3N.

I quite agree. The answer to this problem is to look at the 3H bidder, then decide.

D-12 LOOK AT THE WHOLE CAST OF CHARACTERS

IMPs	Not Vulnerable vs. Vulnerable [BW 101]
You Hold:	♠ K9xx ♥ AJ98xx ♦ -- ♣ 7xx

The Bidding:	P P 1C 1N
	   2H 3D* P 3N
	  ??

* 3D alerted as forcing	

What call would you make on this hand?

Here is a hand where you not only scope out your opponents – it looks like they have had a misunderstanding – but you should look very carefully at your partner. If you are playing with a person who doesn't believe in opening light in third seat, then you probably have a clear double. If you are playing with a normal partner, assuming such exits, who might open a little light in third seat but probably draws the line at having at least ten points, you might also consider peacefully defending, especially if you think your left hand opponent, a passed hand, is unlikely to have seven diamonds.

If you are playing with a very aggressive player, known far and wide for his ultra-light third seat lead-directing opening bids, might well want to take the save If you are going to bid, I believe starting with four clubs is clearly best. A good poker player often makes a probing bet to test the waters and to get a feel for the table. This is done to check how the opponents will react. Your partner just might have good clubs.

There are some hands where your left hand opponent (LHO) might not double four clubs when passed around to him (for example, if he merely has ace-other). Or because of the vulnerability, your LHO might choose to bid one more.

However, if 4C does get doubled, especially with relish, as your sensors detect, you probably should run to 4D and SOS redouble which tells your partner to choose between hearts and lesser spades. He might also return to clubs – having been warned. The expert panel chose to bid four-diamond, choice of majors; but if you decide to bid on this hand, instead of defending, I think trying 4C first is slightly better.

Once again, the bottom line with a hand like this usually depends heavily on the whole cast of characters, including you and your table image.

D-13 LOOK FOR KEY TELLS

IMPs	Neither Vulnerable [BW 1098]
You Hold:	♠ A10
	♥ xxxx
	♦ K10
	♣ J1098x
The Bidding:	1S X P ??

What call would you make with this hand?

There are hands where you look around the table just to evaluate the general caliber of your opponents and then go one way or the other. But there are some hands where, just as in poker, you must get inside the mind of your opponent and guess what he is most likely to do next.

In the above hand, eighteen experts voted to bid 2H; six voted to bid 3H. What would you bid and why?

Bidding 2C or 3C would not be considered in the mainstream of modern bridge bidding because your partner's take-out double tends to focus first and foremost on the other major. And indeed your first priority is to find the heart fit if it exists. But partner's take-out double does not guarantee four hearts; there is merely a reputable presumption that he has four hearts. If you bid three hearts and your partner has only three hearts, you could be too high and in trouble.

Thus if there were no other extenuating circumstances, I would generally agree with the majority that 2H is by far the best bid. You find your heart fit, if there is one, at a safe level. If the opponents compete in spades, as expected, you plan to bid 3C and probably get to the best contract. Note that if your partner happens to have three hearts and three clubs, he should pass 3C since you wouldn't bid 3C if you had five hearts.

If you are playing against weak or very non-aggressive players, I would bid 2H.

But there is a definite and foreseeable problem on this hand. If you look around the table and see that you are playing against good opponents or aggressive opponents, then there is another very big consideration. How do you explain the fact that your RHO did not raise spades? If RHO had three or more spades, over a take-out double he would probably bid 2S even on very few points.

Note the presence of a vacuum here! The lack of a spade raise when you have only two spades and your partner rates to be short means something! Either your partner has a big no-trump type hand (eighteen points or more) or, more likely, your right hand opponent has a lot of spades – perhaps even seven or more.

Most often, your partner's take-out double has short spades, usually two or less. You do not have to provide for the possibility of his having the big hand, because then he would bid again. If he has a relatively normal take-out double, even with some extra values, what will happen if LHO bids 3S over your 2H bid? Your partner certainly will not have a bid, since you could have nothing, and you will have to pass or bid 4C – either of which could be quite wrong.

The best answer to this problem is that you should bid 2H unless you detect that your left hand opponent is about to jump in spades. You should instead bid 3H and your side will be much better positioned over the 3S (or 4S) bid.

You should not only look around the table, you should study LHO under a microscope. Is that the face of a man who is about to jump in spades? Does he have that good seven-card spade suit look? In the poker world, my coauthor of *Poker at The Millennium*, Mike Caro, wrote the definitive textbook on tells (*Caro's Book of Poker Tells*) which are the facial expressions and body signs that indicate how a player feels about his hand.

Many good poker players believe that they can often detect or sense what their opponents are holding. On a bridge hand such as this, it would be extremely helpful if you could anticipate whether your left hand opponent is about to make a strong jump bid in spades.

Once upon a time, I was playing against Freddy Sheinwold, the cofounder of the Kaplan-Sheinwold System, at the annual New England KO Championships which were then held at the Norwich Inn, merely a few miles down Connecticut Route 2 from where Foxwoods is now located.

Freddy was in an aggressive game which merely required him to pick up queen fourth of trumps. Having cashed the trump ace on dummy with each of us following, he then led the jack of spades to which I smoothly played my second spade. He then thought for several minutes, ostensibly thinking about whether to finesse or play for the drop, but, actually studying both my wife and I for tells.

Kathie was just sitting there like someone who didn't know what was going on, and I attempted to look casual like a man who didn't have the queen. He saw through my ruse and took the finesse – losing to Kathie's queen doubleton. So there you have it. There certainly are tells – but let the buyer beware.

D-14 LOOK FOR MAVERICKS

IMPs	Vulnerable vs. Not Vulnerable [ACBL 0104]		
You Hold:	♠ Ax ♥ K ♦ AQJxxx ♣ QJ10x		
The Bidding:	1D 1S ??	2H	4S

What call would you make?

This is a very hard problem and will be even harder if you have no specific partnership agreements about such situations, such as, whether a pass is forcing after a two-over-one response – which shows ten or more points and is not forcing to game.

The expert panel cast ten votes for double, which many suggested was not purely for penalty. But unless you have specifically discussed bidding over competitive 4S bids, it seems likely that partner will interpret your double that you are casting your vote to defend four spades. What would you bid with ♠QJx ♥x ♦KQxxx ♣Axxx? If you pass, your partner might well bid 5H?

Three panelists voted for the pass, which they considered forcing (most panelists consider pass not 100% forcing); and three panelist voted for 4N, which one expert argued should not be Blackwood – but most panelist consider 4N as key card Blackwood for hearts, the last bid suit.

When the opponents preempt and create a problem situation, you are forced to make a guess. Whatever you decide to do could be wrong. For example, on this hand, if you choose to double (the popular choice), your partner might well leave the double in with a hand which would easily make a slam opposite your hand; for example, ♠xx ♥Axxxx ♦Kx ♣Hxxx, where H is ace or king of clubs. Even a relatively bad hand will have some play for slam; for example, ♠xx ♥AQ10xxx ♦xx ♣K9x would make 6D on a finesse with no bad splits.

You have to guess anyway, so why not play a little poker and try to increase your chances of success? Especially if one or both of your opponents look like, or are known to be, very aggressive players, perhaps you should try to turn the tables and give your opponents a problem.

For example, suppose you know that both of your opponents are very aggressive players who bid a lot, and you confidently bid 6D! It might make. Even if it would go down, either of the frisky opponents might guess to take the save.

When you add up the percentages of either the slam making or an opponents taking the save, your total chances of success might well be better with the gambling slam bid than with one of the more conservative ambiguous bids.

In poker, throwing the gauntlet back at the opponents is often the best all-around percentage play. For example, you might make a large bet in a speculative situation. Your chances of ending up with the best hand are supplemented by the possibility that your opponent will fold a hand that would have beaten yours.

D-15 HELL BENT

MATCHPOINTS	Neither Vulnerable
You Hold: ♠ Q10x	
♥ Jx	
♦ KJ9xxx	
♣ xx	

The Bidding:	1H	X	2C*	X**
	P	2D	??	

If You Pass (continuation): P   3C
P   3N   ??

* xfer to diamonds (alerted)
** alerted as responsive X (??)

Assuming you pass out the hand, what do you lead?

The theme of this hand is the question of what you should do if the opponents are clearly on the wrong wave length. Note well that although you strongly suspect that the opponents are much too weak to be playing 3N, unless they can run many club tricks, you should not double as they might run to 4C which might make. Also, you were correct not to double 2D which might have disclosed the error.

You strongly suspect that double of 2C was intended as penalty – not responsive as alerted by other opponent. And opponents 3C was probably intending to play, not inviting 3N. You are playing Capp/1MX, Cappelletti over one-of-a-major doubled, where your 2C bid was a transfer to diamonds and was duly alerted by your partner – although right hand opponent (RHO) apparently misunderstood.

Note that RHO apparently bid 2D because he thought partner's double was responsive. Then he bid 3N over partner's

3C cue bid. Oddly enough, even though they had only twenty-one points between them, 3N was not that bad a contract.

So what would you lead?

You should not lead your fourth best diamond since RHO probably has four or more hence your partner is probably short in diamonds – he chose not to bid diamonds over 2C doubled. You should lead jack of hearts, partner's suit, even though it might give up a trick. The timing in no trump is often very critical.

If you lead anything but a heart, they will make 3N! If you lead a diamond, they will make an overtrick. If you lead jack of hearts, they will go down two. LHO did have a long club suit as suspected.

In many opponent-mix-up situations, it is important to try to figure out what the mistake tells you and/or try to interpret the erroneous bid. Here the inopportune 2D bid should warn you off bidding or leading diamonds. Once you glean what is really going on, you may be able to find the best course of action.

D-16 LOOK BEFORE YOU SAVE

MATCHPOINTS	Both Vulnerable [Goldman Pairs NYC]
You Hold: ♠ xx ♥ AKJxx ♦ KQxx ♣ xx	
The Bidding: 1H X 3D* 4S ??	
* fit showing jump (shows 6-9 points, diamond length and heart fit)	

What call would you make with this hand?

There are several bidding concepts involved in this hand, but none of those concepts is as important as looking around the table. First, I'll discuss the bridge concepts.

When there are two-suit fits, as there certainly are in this hand, you tend to favor offense. Here you know that your partner has at least three hearts and five or more diamonds. Your king and queen of diamonds are great on offense (in the red suits) but may take zero tricks on defense. Because of your informative methods, you may be one of the few players holding your hand who knows the true value of your king and queen fourth of diamonds.

Also, you usually don't save on the five-level if the opponents may go down. You have to question whether the opponents actually may go down. With that in mind, take a good look at the opponent and recall the manner that he bid 4S.

The bottom line is if the 4S bidder has ten or eleven cards in the black suits, they will probably make 4S. But if the ace and king of both red suits cash, they will go down, in which case you should not be saving.

The big question here is whether or not the 4S bidder usually has his bids – or does he tend to bid a lot? We know that he is bidding mostly on shape, not points.

I looked at the guy more carefully. Nothing unusual about his appearance or eyes. Yes, he looked like a man who would probably have his bids. Probably 5-5 or 6-4. He looked back at me casually.

My best guess was that they were going to make it, but we were vulnerable. Would a save go for too many? If you put partner on either four hearts or queen third and the ace of diamonds fifth or sixth, then you certainly have a good save (minus 500) at the five level against their 620 or 650.

Note that most other pairs will not be taking the save since using standard methods, most of the other pairs will merely support hearts and will not disclose the double fit.

One final poker reason to take the 5H save, is that either opponent might take the push to 5S. I bid 5H. They doubled. I went for 500 as advertised. They were on for a normal 620 make in 4S, and we received a very good match point score.

SECTION E
THE AMORPHOUS CUE BID

INTRODUCTION – A COAT OF MANY COLORS

Once upon a time during the olden days of bridge, there came to pass a rule that a cue bid of the opponent's suit promised first round control of that suit. Charles Goren declared in *The Fundamentals of Contract Bridge* (1950), "When either partner makes a bid in the opponent's suit, it indicates the ability to win the first trick of that suit, either with the ace or by trumping."

As time passed and bridge evolved, it became clear that on too many hands, especially in preemptive competition, there wasn't a satisfactory bid available to show a strong hand, which did not have first-round control of the opponent's suit.

The first step, circa early 50s, was to lessen the stringent first round control requirement of the cue bid to second round control. Thus the cue bid of the opponent's suit then either promised either the king of the opponent's suit – or the ace as before – or a singleton in opponent's suit.

The final stage in the evolution (some would say deterioration) of the cue bid came about logically. Since a cue bid no longer promised first round control, why must it promise at least second round control? Why not use the cue bid as an all-purpose flexible strength showing bid? In fact, sometimes the cue bid need not even show extra strength. Sometimes, it might simply be used as a catch-all bid of convenience when there is nothing else to bid.

For example, you opened a minor with a minimum hand. One or both opponents have bid spades. Your partner has made a forcing 3H bid. Now it is your bid and you have no heart fit, no spade stopper and no reason to bid four-of-a-minor, which you would have been forced to bid in old-fashioned bridge. In modern bridge, since you have nothing else to bid and since you do not want to by pass 3N – your partner may have a stopper – you simply cue bid 3S. Partner realizes that you probably would have bid 3N with a spade stopper.

Oswald Jacoby and I once had a discussion about how the cue bid in modern bridge has become somewhat analogous to the all-purpose raise in poker. There are numerous situation at poker where you have a dubious hand, but raising is clearly the most flexible action. In the following pages you will find a number of examples of the modern flexible amorphous cue bid. But in many of those examples, there was simply nothing better to bid.

E-1 TWO CLASSIC CUE BID HANDS

You Hold:	♠ --
	♥ KJxxx
	♦ KQJx
	♣ AJ10x
The Bidding: 1H	1S ??

What call would you make with this hand?

Yes – this is certainly a 2S cue bid by everyone's standards. Anticipating that hearts will be trumps, this hand not only has first round control of spade, it has excellent trump support and strong holdings in each of the side suits.

Charles Goren and Helen Sobel cue bid their way to the cold grand slam which was not bid at the other table, thus resulting in a sizable pickup. In those days, hands were scored using total points as in rubber bridge.

To do the job, you need the right tools. But exactly what are the right tools? Depends on the job. On certain hands, especially those with voids, cue bids showing first-round control are very effective and are often the best tools for accurate slam bidding. Note that Blackwood is often ineffective on such hands.

About fifteen years earlier, in the formative days of bridge, another famous mixed pair, Eli Culbertson and his wife, Josephine, used classic cue bidding to arrive at a grand slam on this freaky hand.

```
                        ♠ AKQ
                        ♥ xx
                        ♦ --
                        ♣ AKQxxxxx
```

The Bidding:
3H	P	P	X
P	3N	P	4C
P	4H	P	4N
P	5H	P	7C

Note that they had the right tools to bid the grand slam which might be difficult to bid using modern day methods:

• The 4C bid over 3N was a natural forcing slam move.

• 4H showed first round control of hearts.

• 4N was not Blackwood, which had not yet been invented at that time; it was a primitive form of DI (the declarative-interrogative 4N) asking partner to show another feature.

• 5H showed second round control of hearts and denied the ace of diamonds.

Although these two classic hands were strong arguments for first-round-control-cue-bids, there are many more hands where the cue bid is needed for general purposes. In the following hands of this section, take note of what you might bid if the cue bid was not available.

E-2 GO WEST YOUNG MAN

You Hold:	♠ x			
	♥ AQx			
	♦ AQJ10xxx			
	♣ xx			
The Bidding:	1S	2C	2D	P
	2S	P	??	

What call would you make with this hand?

Sometimes at the poker table you know generally what you are trying to accomplish but are not sure which of several approaches will yield the best result. In such situations, it seems logical to take the most flexible or noncommittal action, one that will keep most of your options open for a later time.

One such poker example is where you hold a very good hand and would like to get as much money into the pot as possible. But if you bet too much, all your opponents might fold. So you check or bet just a small amount, awaiting further developments. Maybe someone else will bet or raise. You certainly intend to bet larger amounts on subsequent rounds of betting.

In the above hand, the two-level 2D bid in competition promised at least ten points and at least 5 diamonds. On your next bid, you would like very much to make a forcing 3D bid, but in standard bridge, a 3D rebid would not be forcing. Your hand is much too strong to make a non-forcing bid.

You do not want to raise your partner with a singleton spade, and you certainly do not want to bid no trump without a stopper. You could jump to four diamonds but that would take you beyond 3N which might be the best, and only makable, game.

In the old days of bridge, a 3C cue bid here would promise first round control of clubs. Fortunately, in modern bridge, the 3C cue bid here would merely say, "I have a strong hand, please do something helpful." The cue bidder might have a strong hand and may be looking for a club stopper in order to play in no trump – as is the case in this hand. Playing game in no trump instead of five of a minor is particularly important at match point scoring.

The modern interpretation of the 3C cue bid here has fully evolved from showing a stopper to looking for a stopper. It is often officially called a Western Cue Bid, defined as looking for a stopper in the opponent's suit. Of course, if partner dutifully bids 3N showing a stopper and then the cue bidder bids on, then perhaps it wasn't a Western Cue Bid after all?

If it was not Western, then what did the cue bid show? Only the bidder knows.

SECTION E

E-3 DELAYED ACTION CUE BID

IMPs	Vulnerable vs. Non Vulnerable			
You Hold:	♠ xx			
	♥ xx			
	♦ Kxx			
	♣ KQ109xx			
The Bidding:	1H	1S	P	2S
	X	P	??	

What call would you make on this hand?

Here is yet another fascinating solution to a tough problem. You did not have quite enough to bid 2C over the 1S overcall.* If it had then gone, pass, pass, reopening double by your partner, you would then have a textbook jump to 3C, showing a good suit and eight or nine points; you are limited to less than ten points since you did not bid over 1S.

The bad news was that your nasty left hand opponent jacked it up to 2S, which took up all your jumping space and changed everything. The good news is that your partner's free bid double over 2S shows a good hand, usually sixteen points or more – but sometimes shaded with good shape.

Since you are forced to bid in this given situation, a 3C bid could be very weak. You have an absolute maximum for your pass of 1S, and indeed, some very aggressive players might have stretched a 2C bid. A mere 3C bid here would be woefully inadequate, since you might easily make a game with this hand.

You could jump to 4C, but that would get you passed 3N; you would strongly prefer not to play game on the five level. If partner had something like queen-fifth of hearts and three aces (only fourteen points – he should have more), then you will probably make 3N but not 5C.

So what should you bid? Since this is in the cue bid chapter, you have probably guessed. If you bid 3S here, your partner will probably interpret it as Western (see previous page) and bid 3N with a spade stopper. If partner bids 4H, well at least you have two hearts and some kings for him. If partner bids 4D you will have to bid 5C, and search for a new partner. It might even make, especially if partner has a stiff spade.

In a situation where no bid is perfect, you essentially have to gamble one way or the other. Since this bidding problem was given as vulnerable at IMPs, where there is a large premium for bidding games, the amorphous cue bid is clearly the percentage action.

* Note that this would be a good hand for Negative Free Bids.

E-4 CUE BID - WHAT ELSE?

IMPs	Both Vulnerable [BW 397]		
You Hold:	♠ Ax		
	♥ xx		
	♦ AQJxx		
	♣ AKJ9		
The Bidding:	1D	P	1S	P
	3C	P	3D	P
	??			

What call would you make with this hand?

Here is another example of why modern bridge evolved so that a cue bid no longer promises first round control, or anything at all of that suit. In the olden days of bridge when it would have been unthinkable to bid 3H with two small hearts, you would probably be forced to bid four or five diamonds with this hand. But 4D is higher than 3N. You would strongly prefer to have a way to get your partner to bid 3N rather than play for eleven tricks in a minor.

Another reason to keep the bidding conveniently low at 3H is if your partner's hand is still unlimited. Since your 3C bid was ostensibly forcing to game, his 3D preference, which might be a false preference, could even have slam potential. So now over 3H, your partner has much more room to complete his bidding than over 4D.

For example, with a heart stopper, he will usually bid 3N. If he bids 3S, then you can bid 4S, which probably shows a doubleton honor. Over 4S, if he has no heart stopper, he can choose between 4S and 5D with some accuracy.

The good news is that whatever partner does over 3H, you are well placed and should have no further problems. The 3H bid is clearly best, whatever it means.

More than half of the expert panel voted to make the nondescript 3H cue bid on this hand. Call it progress.

E-5 WHEN ALL ELSE FAILS

IMPs	Vulnerable vs. Non Vulnerable [BW 599]		
You Hold:	♠ A ♥ x ♦ AQxxxx ♣ AJxxx		
The Bidding:	1D 3C ??	1H P	P 3H	P P

What call would you make with this hand?

What's going on with partner? What does his 3H cue bid show after he originally passed ?

He might have a penalty pass of hearts. Since a double of one heart would be negative, if he had a heart stack, he would check hoping that partner (you) would reopen with a double. But now that you have reopened with a jump, he is showing something good. But what?

Generally, his hand must fall into one of two categories. Either he has a penalty pass of the one heart overcall, in which case he is virtually unlimited, or he has a hand too weak to bid over 1H but which has been reevaluated in light of your bidding. In this latter case, he either has a nice fit with one or both of your suits, or perhaps has some useful values in diamonds or clubs. There probably is some remote chance that he had an awkward hand that had no good bid over 1H, and now he is trying to get you to bid 3N with a heart stopper (Western style).

How do you find out what he has?

Answer: One dubious cue bid deserve another. Try bidding 3S. What does it mean? If it means you have first round control of spades, as in the old days of bridge. Your main objective here is to see what partner will bid to shed light on his previous actions.

E-6 THE AMORPHOUS SLAM TRY

MATCHPOINTS	Vulnerable vs. Non Vulnerable [BW 302]
You Hold: ♠ K98xxx ♥ Q ♦ Q10 ♣ 109xx	

The Bidding:	2H	P	4H	X
	P	4S	P	5D
	P	?		

What call would you make with this hand?

Five diamonds is to play and shows a big hand. It is not a cue bid in support of spades. At this point, the 5D bidder may not have any spade support at all, or he may have some support for spades along with his diamonds. Partner's double followed by 5D shows a hand too good to simply bid 5D. He has a solid seventeen points or more.

Although you have no outside cards, you certainly have another bid coming. Your 4S bid could have been a very weak hand. Partner might easily have AQx of spades, AK long of diamonds and A of clubs (seventeen points). But he could have a better hand with the wrong cards, and you would not make a slam. For example, if partner has KQ of clubs instead of the ace, then you would be off two cashing aces.

What bid can you make here which might get you to a makable slam but also might allow you to stop? When you want to bid on, but you are not quite sure what to bid, what do you do?

You guessed it. Bid 5H and see what partner does. If he bids only 5S, you should pass. If partner bids 6D, you probably have several tricks for him.

If partner bids 5N, he probably has reasonably good spades and wants you to pick a slam. Partner certainly should not expect you to have better than king sixth of spades. You would clearly prefer 6S to 6D, because in diamonds partner might have trouble using your hand.

An expert panel chose 5H as the best bid on this hand.

E-7 FURTHER OUT WEST

You Hold:	♠ xx		
	♥ Axxx		
	♦ Qxx		
	♣ Qxxx		
The Bidding:	1D	1S	X	P
	3D	P	??	

What call would you make on this hand?

Your partner has jumped to 3D showing a healthy opening bid and a long diamond suit. If partner had merely the AK seventh of diamonds and a spade stopper, you might make 3N. Partner actually has more strength than that, but he might not have a spade stopper. Although you only have eight points, that might well be enough to make a 3N game if your partner has a spade stopper. How can you find out?

What do you do when you think your side has enough strength to play game in no trump but you do not have a stopper in the opponent's bid suit? There is a slight variation of the Western Cue Bid theme which has become a standard solution to this kind of problem.

In many game-going auctions where you lack a stopper in the opponent's bid suit, you can make a convenient cue bid and hope that your partner has a stopper and can bid 3N. In modern bridge, in this type of situation, your cue bid does not show a stopper. Nor does it necessarily show any extra values. All you need is enough strength (points) to make a game possible in light of your partner's bidding. And partner knows that if you had a stopper, then you might well have bid the 3N yourself.

There are numerous occasions in poker where you make an amorphous bet, a small amount, to see what your opponents will do and how they do it. In bridge, sometimes it's best to make the cheapest convenient bid, just to see what happens.

E-8 THE ALL PURPOSE CUE BID

IMPs	Both Vulnerable [BW 1201]
You Hold:	♠ AQxx
	♥ Axxx
	♦ Jx
	♣ xxx
The Bidding:	P 1C 1D P
	??

What call would you make with this hand?

When this hand was presented to the expert panel, a great majority of experts voted for the cue bid which normally shows three card or more trump support.

Although this cue bid normally shows a limit raise or better in partner's suit, here diamonds; because you have such an excellent passed hand, you are willing to promote your jack-doubleton of diamonds. Your eleven points are all prime quality points, two and one-half honor tricks.

Even though you only have two diamonds, as opposed to the usual requisite three or more, partner will definitely not complain about your hand when you put it down as dummy. And if, on a good day, partner happens to bid two-of-a-major, you have a delightful raise to three.

This cue bid does it all. It tells your partner that you have ten or eleven points – you can not have more since you are a passed hand. It also shows that you have support for both unbid suits and you even have some support for your partner's suit.

This is a bid that has practically no down side.

E-9 THE DO SOMETHING CUE BID

MATCHPOINTS	Vulnerable Vs. Not Vulnerable [BW 1201]		
You Hold: ♠ 98xx ♥ -- ♦ KJ109 ♣ Axxxx			
The Bidding: 1N	P	2C	3H
P	P	P	??

What call would you make with this hand?

A great majority of the expert panel chose the 4H cue bid on this hand.

Although you only have eight high card points, in view of the fact that the three heart bidder probably has most of the heart high cards, your partner's strong no trump probably contains mostly working or useful cards for you. If your partner has something like ♠Axx ♥Jxx ♦AQxx ♣KQx (sixteen points), he might make twelve tricks in diamonds by ruffing two hearts.

Even though you might make a slam if partner has the right hand for you, you should not even think about bidding a slam with such a minimum point count. You should be perfectly content to get to a comfortable game. Since you have some shape, it is quite possible that other suits are splitting badly.

The bottom line here is that the best reason for making any bid is that it will allow partner to get to a good contract. If you bid 4H on this hand, partner will have to bid his best suit. And lo and behold, that will probably be your best contract.

This is clearly one of the hands where your point count is secondary to your distribution.

E-10 THE LEAST OF EVILS CUE BID

IMPs	Neither Vulnerable [BW 400]
You Hold:	♠ Ax
	♥ AQxx
	♦ Qxx
	♣ AKxx
The Bidding:	1C 3D 3S P
	??

What would you bid with this hand?

When this hand was presented to an expert bidding panel, the vast majority chose the 4D cue bid, notwithstanding that the hand lacks first or second round control of diamonds.

The real problem here is that all other bids describe the hand worse. Three no trump will probably make, but your hand is too strong to sign off in game. If your partner has six good spades and a short diamond, you should have good play for a slam. If you bid 4H, partner should play you for hearts and clubs, and might even pass.

This hand is a prime example of the amorphous cue bid, in that it exemplifies how the cue bid has deteriorated, in the eyes of some of the older Culberson era players, from first round control to second round control to no control at all. In modern bridge we now acknowledge the concept of the all-purpose cue bid, for truly, that is what it has become.

There are certain analogies between the strong sounding cue bid at bridge and the all-purpose strong sounding raise at poker. Once upon a time, a raise at poker usually showed a good hand, or perhaps a bluff. Nowadays, more sophisticated poker players tend to slow play or trap with very good hands; an immediate raise, especially after the flop, is often merely a tactical weapon, information probe, or inhibitory attempt.

E-11 DISCLOSING THE PENALTY PASS

IMPs	Both Vulnerable		
You Hold:	♠ AJ98x		
	♥ xx		
	♦ Qx		
	♣ KQxx		
The Bidding:	1H	1S	P	P
	2C	P	??	

What call would you make with this hand?

Although this hand started out as a defensive misfit, by not reopening with the usual double, your partner has suddenly told you that he does not want to defend spades – presumably because he has singleton or void. The 2C bid tends to show a light opening bid, perhaps based on distribution.

What should you bid? Although you would like to raise clubs, no club bid does justice to your hand. You are too good for 3C (invitational). And it would not be wise to bid 4C, which would show less values and more shape. Enter the all-purpose cue bid. Partner will not be sure whether you have the penalty pass hand or just the scattered unbidable values hand.

If over your 2S cue bid, partner bids 3C, you will raise to 4C and leave it up to partner. If partner bids 3D, which might be a three card fragment, you will happily bid 3N. If partner bids 3H, you have to guess whether or not to try four. I would probably pass 3H because of the inferences from his 2C bid.

Finally, if partner bid 3S, one cue bid deserves another, presumably to find out what I'm all about, I would bid 4C rather than 3N. If partner then stops in 4C, it might be the best spot. Note that if neither of us has a strong preference about the hands, the bidding might stop abruptly.

E-12 CUE BID SPECIFICALLY SHOWS TWO SUITS

MATCHPOINTS	Neither Vulnerable [WBL 1103]
You Hold: ♠ x ♥ AK10xx ♦ AK ♣ AKxxx	
The Bidding: 3D ??	

What call would you make with this hand?

You have a huge hand which you can not adequately describe to partner. If you double, partner will probably bid spades and then nothing you do will show your two long suits and shortness in spades. If you follow up your double with a new suit, partner will play you for a one-suiter and will pass or revert to spades hoping you have tolerance. Thus, you should not start with a double.

Although most of the hands in this section demonstrated the flexibility, if not outright ambiguous nature of the modern cue bid, there is at least one situation in modern bridge where the meaning of the cue bid does not vary.

Most experts play that an immediate cue bid over a preempt, especially if the cue bid is higher than 3N, is a two-suited hand. Normally the auctions, 3C 4C or 3D 4D show five-five or better in the majors – hence the cue bidder's partner usually bids his better major. But if over responder's major suit bid, the cue-bidder now bids the other minor, then that shows the remaining two suits and responder should pass or correct.

Note that some partnerships have attempted to further refine cue-bidding to show specific two suiters, often at the expense of giving up 4N as Blackwood.

E-13 BIG TWO-SUITER

IMPS	Vulnerable vs. Not Vulnerable [BW 502]
You Hold:	♠ AKQxx ♥ AQ ♦ x ♣ AK10xx
The Bidding: 2H	P 4H ??

What call would you make with this hand?

Hands like this make you appreciate having discussed what cue bids after preempts mean.

You certainly cannot afford to double with this hand. Partner will most likely respond with 5D and then your 5S bid would show a big hand with spades. Certainly it would not show spades and clubs. Partner would probably pass with hands containing short spades and four clubs.

A 5H cue bid here shows a powerful two suiter. Your partner should look at his hand and decide whether he tolerates spades, if that is one of your suits, or not.

If he can not tolerate spades (two or less), he should bid 5N to find out which minor you have. You might have a partnership agreement that a 6C bid here, is either better or worse than the 5N bid.

Note again that many experienced partnerships have further conventionalized two-suit cue bidding auctions after preempts. But due to the lack of bidding space and only a few bids available to show different hands, there are limits as to how much can be accomplished.

E-14 LEAPING COMPLIMENT

MATCHPOINTS	Neither Vulnerable
You Hold: ♠ xxx	
♥ Kxxxx	
♦ Qx	
♣ Jxx	
The Bidding: 2S 3S P ??	

What call would you make if you are playing Liberalized Leaping Michaels?

When the opponents open a weak two bid against you, much of your side's needed bidding space has been taken away. There are many hands that you would like to describe, but only a limited number of bids available. It would be wise to adopt several modern methods to help your side compete effectively.

If your partnership now uses Libralized Leaping Michaels (*Cross Reference: see A-17*), you can show a two-suited competitive hand with the other major and a minor by jumping to the four-level of the minor. But how do you show both minors? You should not play that 2N over a weak 2S is unusual, since you need 2N to distinguish between a strong balanced hand and a take-out double. But you can add minor two-suiters as another hand showed by the cue bid.

Before we state what you should bid with the above hand, let us discuss the three possible hands that your partner might have for his 3S cue bid:

1. He might have a big hand or a lot of tricks and all he needs to make 3N is for you to have a spade stopper (much like Western cue bid)

2. He might have a two-suiter with the minor suits

3. He might have a two-suiter with the other major and a minor that is good enough to force to game (note that a Leaping Michaels jump to four-of-a-minor is not forcing).

In view of what partner might have for his 3S bid, your first obligation is to bid 3N with a spade stopper. If partner then pulls 3N to four-of-a-suit, then that shows one of the two-suiters discussed above.

If you do not have a stopper in the cue-bid suit, then you should bid your best minor. Your partner will have five-five or better in the minors much more frequently than the other two holdings. But if over your four-of-a-minor, your partner bids four of the other major, then he indeed has the big forcing-to-game two suiter described above.

Once again, the cue-bid which once had a very specific meaning, is now used to show several different hands in modern bridge.

E-15 AVOID AMORPHOUS CUE FOR MORE SPECIFIC BID

MATCHPOINTS	Neither Vulnerable [ACBL 503]		
You Hold: ♠ 10xx ♥ K10 ♦ AQJxx ♣ AJx			
The Bidding: 1S 4H	P P	2D ??	3H

What call would you make with this hand?

You have fifteen high card points, but your king of hearts is a very questionable value. Your partner has a good hand but his 4H cue bid does not promise a heart control (first or second round), though he might well be counting a heart shortness as part of his values. Since he was not forced to bid – he could have passed or bid 4D, his 4H cue bid should have extra values.

A majority of the expert panel chose the five club cue bid. Perhaps it is a matter of one amorphous cue bid deserves another, but then who would know what is going on? I agree that it probably shows the ace of clubs rather than a second suit, though you might hold 6-5 or even 5-5. But 5C bypasses 4N and just about precludes the possibility of bidding a cold grand. For example, if partner has long solid spades, heart void and king of diamonds. Also, looking at your hand, you know that there are a number of hands where 6D makes but 6S goes down. For example, on a heart lead or when partner has ♠AKxxx ♥x ♦Kxx ♣KQxx.

Assuming that you are playing partner for fifteen points plus, you would be well advised to bid Blackwood and get some concrete information about the three missing key cards, including diamond king – last bid suit, or two key cards with a void. If he has all three, then you bid 5N, showing all key cards, and he bids seven with solid spades.

E-16 MAKE MOST DESCRIPTIVE BID

MATCHPOINTS	Both Vulnerable [ACBL 602]
You Hold: ♠ AQ98xx ♥ -- ♦ AJxx ♣ Axx	
The Bidding: 1S 2C X P ??	

What call would you make with this hand?

When this hand was presented to an expert panel, twice as many experts voted for the 3C cue bid as the 3D bid, which was my choice. Although the cue bid does show a good hand, I think that the cue bid is very inappropriate here. It only works out if partner then bids one of your suits (spades or diamonds) which is unlikely. If partner make the rather likely 3H bid over 3C, you must bid 3S, which will probably lead to playing 3N or 4S.

But you might be cold for 6D! If partner has good diamond support, you might be cold for 6D and going down in 4S, for example, ♠xx ♥QJxxx ♦KQxxx ♣x. I see no theoretical flaws in a 3D bid. If the hand is a great misfit and partner passes 3D, it is probably your best contract – you only have fifteen points.

If partner bids 3H, certainly a likely possibility, your 3S rebid describes your hand very well. If partner raises 3D to 4D or 5D, there is much to be said for shooting out 6D! Note that partner's raise to 4D bypasses 3N, which he would be unlikely to do with more values in hearts than diamonds – he might bid 3H to stay under 3N.

It seems the jump to 3D is a do-everything bid and describes your hand very well. I would avoid making the ambiguous amorphous cue bid in this situation.

Quite simply, the general rule is that you make the non-descriptive cue bid when you are looking for no trump or you have no better descriptive bid. Here 3D is a vastly superior bid both when partner is strong or with a weak misfit.

INTRODUCTION - PSYCHIC BIDS

To most of the world, the game of poker is synonymous with bluffing. When non-poker players talk about playing poker in a given situation, they are usually talking about bluffing. Many confrontations, on many levels, are settled after a lot of intimidating big talk. But is it just talk? Is someone bluffing?

In contract bridge, aggressive players often do not have appropriate values for their bids – especially their preemptive bids. Sometimes these aggressive bids are completely outrageous distortions of what normally would be expected – sometimes even bold-faced lies! These exaggerated or false bids at bridge which are very similar to bluffing at poker are often called psychic bids* because of their psychological impact. So let the opponents beware. It is widely held that you should always take your opponent's bidding with a grain of salt.

It is all well and good and even Marquis of Queensbury to attempt to deceive the opponents at bridge and perhaps trick them out of bidding their games and slams. But there is usually some amount of risk. Sometimes you get caught! That is the major down side.

When you bluff at poker, sometimes you get caught for a big loss. When you make a psychic bid at bridge, sometimes you get doubled and pay a big penalty. These are understandable occupational hazards. But there is yet another interesting consideration in bluffing at bridge! Sometimes your partner gets you!

Your partner, who also heard your psychic bid, is ethically obligated to make appropriate bids based on his hand – which may result in a disaster for your side. Also, because of your psychic bid, your partner may make an abnormal lead which costs dearly. Although your partner is normally on your side, if you make a psychic bid, you often have three opponents at the table instead of the usual two. If you are considering bluffing at the bridge table, remember that you must also consider the possibility of your partner going wrong as part of the down side.

Although blatant outright psyches generally are much less frequent today in modern bridge than they were in the lively formative years of bridge (30s and 40s), occasional psyches are still a valuable and colorful tool found in the reserve arsenals of most experts.

* The term "psychic bid" was initially coined in 1931 by Dorothy Sims (wife of P. Hal Sims) to mean "create an illusion of strength" or to "conceal weakness."

F-1 "APPEARANCES BLUFF" AT BRIDGE

MATCHPOINTS	Vulnerable vs. Non-Vulnerable
You Hold: ♠ Axx ♥ xx ♦ Ax ♣ AKQ10xx	
The Bidding: 2N 3H P P ??	

What call would you make with this hand?

I had the good fortune to make one of the most obvious poker bluff bids that I have ever made while playing with the master himself, Ozzie Jacoby, to whom this book is dedicated, in a National Men's Pairs event.

On the above hand, I opened a slightly offbeat 2N. When 3H was passed around to me, I knew that Ozzie had very little and it appeared that my left hand opponent (LHO) might be making 3H or even more. With my almost-sure eight solid tricks, I was not inclined to sell out, but I did not particularly want to bid 4C on the four level where I might have five losers.

I reasoned that if my LHO, who was an experienced player, had a solid suit to the ace-king-queen long, he probably would have passed, hoping to cash many tricks against a no-trump contract. He was probably missing at least one heart honor.

I bid a confident 3N. My LHO, looking at ace-king-jack seventh of hearts, quite naturally assumed that I probably had queen-third of hearts. Hence it was only a question of which wrong thing he would do. Note that he would not lead the ace or king of hearts intending to shift, because his partner might well have only one heart.

If LHO had chose to lead any other suit attempting to find an entry to his partner's hand, I would have simply cashed out eight tricks, down one, for a good score against hearts which made four at most of the other tables.

Not at our table! After some thought, LHO decided to bid 4H. After ruffing the second round of clubs, declarer played one high trump, fetching the ten from Ozzie who had started with queen-ten doubleton. Then declarer maneuvered to get to dummy and took the losing heart finesse (queen would have dropped) for down one.

At supper between sessions, Ozzie noted that I had used an appearances bluff on that hand. He compared it to a poker bluff aided by appearances that he had executed during World War II in Hawaii against a Navy Captain playing pot-limit five-card stud. Ozzie had a ten-nine-eight showing and was dealt a queen for his last card. Ozzie bet the pot and the Captain folded assuming that Ozzie had been playing for a two-way straight with a jack as his hole card. The Captain was right about playing for the two-way straight, but Ozzie actually had a seven in the hole.

F-2 BLUFFING AT BRIDGE

IMP PAIRS	Neither Vulnerable [Cavendish Calcutta]
You Hold: ♠ AQJ10xxx ♥ x ♦ A10xxx ♣ --	
The Bidding: 4H 4S 5H 6D P ??	

What call would you make with this hand?

One of the greatest and most dramatic poker bluff bids of all time was made by Gaylor Kasle on this hand while playing in one of the few big money bridge tournaments – The Cavendish Club Invitational Tournament, originally held at the Cavendish Club in New York, but has since moved to Las Vegas.

Although Gaylor knew that he had a heart loser, he chose to bid 7D on the theory that his expert opponent would assume that he had first round control of hearts for his raise to seven. His bluff worked!

Bob Hamman, one of the world's greatest and highest ranked players, on lead with ♠9xxxx ♥AQ10xxx ♦-- ♣ xx, assumed that Gaylor had to have the heart void for his voluntary seven bid and did not lead his Ace, which would have cashed. Thus, the grand slam made for a huge swing at IMP pairs.

SEQUEL

About six months later, after the hand had made the rounds by word of mouth, the hand was given as an opening lead problem in *Bridge World*, February 2001. Twelve of the thirty expert panelists chose to lead the ace of hearts. What would you have led?

F-3 BASIC BLUFFING - PSYCHING 101

MATCHPOINTS	Not Vulnerable vs. Vulnerable
You Hold: ♠ xxxx	
♥ KQx	
♦ xxx	
♣ xxx	
The Bidding: ??	

Need we ask if you would bid on this hand in first seat?

Before going further into bluffing/psyching at bridge, perhaps a couple of flashbacks, as seen through my own eyes, might help put psyching into perspective.

Many years ago when I was first getting into bridge, I often played with a fellow MIT student who was an ardent disciple of the Kaplan-Sheinwold system. In addition to weak no-trumps (11-14 points), the K-S System then included controlled psyches, which were defined as opening the bidding in first or second seat with three to six points all in the suit opened.

On this particular occasion, after my partner had opened (psyched) with one heart, I just happened to hold a perfect weak-jump shift (also part of K-S), consisting mainly of the ace-queen sixth of clubs. Neither of the somewhat timid opponents chose to bid, and I played the hand undoubled down three for a match point top, as the opponents were cold for five hearts.

Even if the opponents had competed, they probably would have played three no-trump which would make only nine tricks with a club lead, and would have also given us an excellent score. It would have been nearly impossible for them to play in their 5-3 heart fit after our one heart opening bid since a three heart bid over my three-club jump shift would have been a cue bid.

F-4 THE PSYCHIC OVERCALL

MATCHPOINTS	Neither Vulnerable [late 30s]
You Hold: ♠ Axx	
♥ xxx	
♦ JTxxx	
♣ xx	
The Bidding: P　　1C　　??	

In the early days of bridge in the 1930s, psychic bids were very fashionable and were considered artistic and sporting. But after a few years and perhaps a few disastrous results, psyching fell out of favor. Then, in the 50s, systems such as Kaplan-Sheinwold, Roth-Stone and Bulldog, introduced the notion of the controlled psyche (*Cross Reference: see F-3*) both for psychic opening bids and psychic overcalls.

I first encountered psychic overcalls while playing rubber bridge at the Boston Chess Club. Occasionally, one of the shrewder players would overcall one-of-a-major on a three-card suit, with mixed results. An octogenarian retired judge, Emil Fuchs, who had once owned the Boston Braves (before they moved to Milwaukee), explained to me that the controlled psychic overcall system, which he had once played, was actually very specific.

The first requirement was that your partner must be a passed hand. You don't want to fool around and obstruct your partner if it is your hand. The second requirement was that you should have less than eight high-card points – thus the opponents should have at least an easy part score. You should also have ace or king-third in the major suit you psyche. If your partner raises, it should be somewhat playable. And if partner leads your suit, at least you have a card there.

Ironically, psychic overcalls worked better in the old days before negative doubles were commonplace. If your left hand opponent doubled you (then for penalties), you could run or redouble to get partner to bid. But a psychic overcaller will find a reopening double on his right very awkward.

I have made the bid several times during the last decade, and each time it produced amusing if not effective results. One time they bid 6N making, which gave them a top because it was normal to play six-of-the-major I had psyched.

The last time I did this, the opponent screamed for the director, pointed his finger at me and said, "This man overcalled a three-card suit!"

I smiled sheepishly and said, "He's right. I did." The director then warned me that I should put "occasional psyches" on my convention card. I pointed to my card where it was already checked. Psychics are very rare these days.

F-5 PSYCHING 102 - THE 1N OVERCALL

IMPs	Not Vulnerable vs. Vulnerable
You Hold:	♠ Jx
	♥ Jx
	♦ Kx
	♣ K98xxxx
The Bidding: P	1D ??

What call would you make on this hand?

Here is a classic move which is particularly effective against weaker players. At the table, instead of the usual 3C (or even 4C) preemptive bid, my partner chose to psyche a 1N overcall, which normally shows 15-17+ high card points! In his usual humorous drawl, he later told me that the hand "looked like a NT hand!"

Note that his fall back position was to run out to clubs if he was doubled in no trump. The conditions that he was not vulnerable against vulnerable and that his partner was a passed hand, also contributed to his decision.

Note well that one of the key considerations in any psychic situation is the danger of your partner acting on your false bid. The main danger in this particular hand was that partner might make a transfer bid and thus get you dangerously high. Also, if partner had a ten point hand with short clubs, and chose to bid 3N, you might get into serious trouble.

As it turned out, the bid worked incredibly well. I chose to bid the *junk Stayman* 2C (for the majors) with my six point hand and four-four in the majors. It then went all pass and the opponents missed a lay down 3N – they had twenty-six points between them. Both the nineteen point opening bidder and seven point responding hand could have taken a bid.

F-6 BLUFFING - GRABBING THEIR SUIT

MATCHPOINTS	Both Non Vulnerable
You Hold: ♠ Axxx	
♥ 10x	
♦ xx	
♣ KQ109x	
The Bidding: 1D 1H P ??	

What would you bid with this hand?

Here is a fairly routine expert move which has no or very little down side. Many players would bid 2C with the above hand, depending somewhat on whether the partnership agreement on new suits over overcalls is forcing, not-forcing but constructive, or undisciplined – although 2C might be bid regardless. And indeed, if you have a club fit (5-3 fit or better), and get to play the hand in clubs, you might get a reasonable match point score if you make exactly 110.

But note that you might make a better match point score by playing in hearts, especially if partner has a good hand which is about 50% likely on this bidding – in light of your right hand opponent's pass. Is there a bid which optimizes your chances of success?

To analyze this situation, start by assuming that your left hand opponent (LHO) either has a weak hand (otherwise undefined) or has a strong penalty pass of hearts. The weak hand is much more likely but your best bid should keep the penalty possibility in mind. If your LHO has about 2-5 points (average), you have nine, the opening bidder has about 11-16 (average), then your partner will usually have about 10-15.

The bottom line is that your side will usually have more high card points than your opponents, but if LHO has a good hand, the points might be roughly equally divided. Because your side probably has the preponderance of strength and because you are playing match points, it would be rare to get a big match point score for playing in a minor. If partner has more than eleven points, you should try to play this hand in hearts or in NT.

One of the biggest disadvantages with bidding 2C is that it bypasses 1N. It is usually better to play 1N (especially not vulnerable) than a minor at matchpoints. Thus your best bid is clearly 1S! Even if LHO has a big (sixteen point plus) hand and doubles 1S (not penalties – shows big hand), your partner might be able to bid 1N or 2H.

If LHO has a normal opener and passes 1S, then your side will play the hand in no trump or a major, and get lots more match points than if you had bid 2C. Finally, if your partner is short in spades, your 1S bid might keep the opponents out of their best spot.

Although I have just spent some number of words on the constructive merits of bidding 1S, it was actually the destructive merits which made the hand newsworthy.

This hand occurred in a New England regional many years ago soon after I had just started playing bridge. In the daily bulletin I was praised for making a brilliant tactical bid which effectively kept the opponents from finding their spade partial which was bid at almost every other table, often making three. We stole the hand in 1N making two after a heart lead. This hand heightened my awareness of the possibility of grabbing the opponent's suit:

North
♠ x
♥ AJxxx
♦ KJxxx
♣ Jx

West
♠ KQ108
♥ K
♦ Axxx
♣ Axxx

East
♠ J987
♥ Q987x
♦ Qx
♣ xx

South
♠ Axxx
♥ 10x
♦ xx
♣ KQ109x

F-7 BLUFFING – STEALING THEIR SUIT

MATCHPOINTS	Both Non Vulnerable
You Hold: ♠ Axx	
♥ 10xx	
♦ Q109x	
♣ xxx	
The Bidding: 1D x ??	

What call would you make with this hand?

While on the subject of grabbing the opponent's suit, let's take a look at one of the oldest poker bids in bridge, psyching a major over a take-out double. Your partner opens with a suit for which you have good support – a home in case you get doubled. The opponent on your right makes a take-out double. You have a weak hand such that game for your side is very unlikely. How many of your partner's suit should you raise preemptively?

One option is to forego the raising and instead make a poker bid. If you bid one of a short major, you may steal that suit. In the above hand, a 1S bid is probably a better choice than 1H on the down side theory. Perhaps the biggest down side of bidding 1S on ace third, is that your partner will occasionally have four spades and raise you, and perhaps even bid a second time. If you choose to stand tall in the pocket and play spades rather than scramble out to your real suit, you will find that ace third plays much better than three small.

In the early days of bridge, the above ploy was so popular that a defense had to be formulated. Even today, many partnerships play that the auction one-of-a-suit, take-out double (usually for majors), one-of-a-major, double. In this context it shows four or more good spades, and enough strength to play games.

Cross Reference: see C-10

F-8 TWO FOR THE PRICE OF ONE

IMPs	Not Vulnerable vs. Vulnerable [ACBL 1003]
You Hold:	♠ QJ9xx ♥ xx ♦ QJ97 ♣ AQ
The Bidding:	1H P 4H ??

What call do you make with this hand?

Nine members of the expert bidding panel chose to pass whereas only four venturesome souls chose to bid 4S. The passers noted quite correctly that you might get doubled and go for a number on a hand where the opponents were going down. The conservative position is that you don't have enough to bid 4S on this hand, so why try to be a hero?

However, I vote strongly with the minority. I think it is a clear cut 4S bid unless there are overriding considerations. For example, if you are far ahead in the match and do not need to win IMPs – simply don't gamble and lose IMPs. Also, if you are playing against novices that you rate to beat anyway, you might want to stay in your chair.

If you are trying to win IMPs, I believe bidding 4S on this hand is an acceptable risk. You will probably run into a big spade stack only about one time in six. If your partner has a singleton heart, he will usually have at least three spades for you and sometimes more. But that is not the main argument!

This is a poker hand! Think of it partly as a bluff. When the bidding goes 1H then 4H, that always means that both opponents are hot to play hearts – at least five in opener's hand and four or five in responder's hand. At least one of the opponents will be unhappy that you bid 4S – and often both of them! Either one of them might take the push to 5H.

When I was first learning the game back in Boston in the 60s, I played several times with a local expert, Bill Butcher, who sarcastically had a rule for this type of situation. He said to always make the two-way bid. It might be right but even if it is wrong, either one or both of the opponents might come riding in to your rescue. "So at least two [chances] for the price of one" he said.

Over the years, I have found that he was right. The poker factor in this type of situation should be a strong consideration in deciding whether or not to take the plunge. It is sort of like in poker, when making a big bet can win in two ways – it is either right or the opponents might do the wrong thing.

On this hand I proudly recommend boldly bidding 4S, and don't let people see that your fingers are crossed. Either opponent might bid 5H.

Since the title of this hand is "Two for the Price of One," allow me to give you a second hand, illustrating a simple variation of this concept that comes up frequently. You hold six little spades, a short heart (singleton or void), and four two with little or no points in the minors.

The bidding again goes 1H X 4H and it is your turn to bid. I have seen this problem put before expert panels numerous times and the conservatives usually prevail, saying that you should pass and not bid 4S unless partner doubles again.

I disagree. If you pass, your partner, who may have fifteen or more points, might not be able to double again. Since he usually has four spades for his take out double, he could easily have something like AKxx in spades. Then right away, you know that this hand will play about six tricks better in spades than in hearts. And If he happens to also fit your side four-card suit, for example, with AQJ over opening bidder, bidding 4S could easily produce a double-game string.

Here is the real good news – the poker factor! Even if he doesn't happen to have the right stuff for you and your bid is essentially wrong, at least one of the opponents is going to have a very short spade holding, and may well decide to bid 5H.

Now you have pushed the opponents up to the five level! Well done. You now hold your breath and hope that your partner knows that the five level belongs to the opponents.

F-9 BLUFF EXTRAORDINAIRE

MATCHPOINTS	Vulnerable vs. Not Vulnerable
You Hold: ♠ xx	
♥ AKQxxxxx	
♦ x	
♣ Qx	
The Bidding: P P 3H ??	

What in the world would you do with this hand?

Many years ago, Peter Leventritt playing with Howard Schenken found himself in this situation. The player on his right was Marty Cohn, well known for his enterprising bids.

What can you do when they bid your long suit?

You can't double because that is for take out and your partner will bid one of your short suits. You can't bid 4H because that would be a cue bid and your partner will bid. You could bid 3N, but that could easily be a match point disaster even if you make it, and one or both of your opponents may have a suit that will run, or your partner may bid because he thinks you have a balanced hand.

Peter made the obligatory pass and hoped that his partner would be short in hearts and might reopen with a double. His partner had a typical passed hand and no reason to bid. They defended three hearts and beat it seven tricks for a match point zero. What could Peter have done? Nothing?

Nothing! There was simply nothing else he could do! Passing was his best chance. If his partner, who rates to be short in hearts, had a few cards and reopened with a double, then Marty would have run to his real suit. Then Peter could have bid 4H to play, after the psyche had been exposed.

I have heard that after the tournament was over, Peter, one of the great gentlemen of the game, approached Marty with outstretched hand and congratulated him on his bold bid. But no one quoted his language for posterity.

I have also heard that Marty coined the phrase, "Good bidding is its own reward."

F-10 BLACKWHAT?

IMPs	Vulnerable vs. Not Vulnerable		
You Hold:	♠ --		
	♥ AKxxxx		
	♦ AKxxxxx		
	♣ --		
The Bidding:	1S	2S	P	3H
	3S	??		

When you pick up a super-freak, there is often room for creativity. In this auction I was tempted to just rear back and bid seven hearts, but there was no guarantee that we had no trump loser, or they might have a cheap save.

Then I had an inspiration. Bid Blackwood and perhaps check for the queen of trumps. Someone might think I actually cared about how many aces we had!

So I bid 4N. My left hand opponent then scared me by bidding 5S. My partner doubled with his J1098 of spades, to warn me that he wanted to defend. But I didn't!

I bid 6H. Can you blame the opener with two aces and the QJx of trumps for doubling? Maybe he thought we had a misunderstanding with our Blackwood responses.

There was no contest. My unhappy partner loved the dummy. Even though he merely had three little hearts and two little diamonds, he ruffed the opening ace, drew two trump, ruffed out the third diamond and claimed conceding only one trump trick, plus 1660. Much better than the − 500 save at the other table which was bid over the jump to 6H.

F-11 CONSTRUCTIVE DOUBLE OF BLACKWOOD

IMPs	Vulnerable vs. Not Vulnerable [Regional Swiss]		
You Hold: ♠ xx			
♥ Axxx			
♦ KQx			
♣ Qxxx			
The Bidding: 2S	3C	4N	??

What call would you make with this hand?

Of course you are quite sure that your right hand opponent (RHO) is fooling around with his 4N, ostensibly Blackwood bid. But does your partner know?

You do have just about enough values to bid and make 5C, assuming your partner has a decent 3C overcall, but why is your RHO jacking it up to 4N? Why did he not just simply bid 4S, since you know he can not possibly have enough to be seriously thinking about slam.

The answer is that he probably suspects that you might make a slam and he is trying to deceive you. Your partner might have a big hand.

Note that if RHO had bid 4S, then you would have simple bid 5C, since you really have nothing else to say. Certainly, you do not have nearly enough to bid 4N.

But now that RHO has bid 4N, what is your best call? Note that over a legitimate 4N Blackwood, you might be bidding 5C on a weak, save-oriented hand with clubs and distribution.

Your correct bid here is the constructive double over what rates to be a 4N psychic bid. This tells partner that you have at least a minimum opening bid in support of clubs. It does not say that you want to double the opponents in 5S. If you want to do that, you simply pass and double later since 4N is a forcing bid.

If your LHO bids 5S and your partner passes, that is an invitational forcing pass, where your partner is asking you to bid a slam if you have extras. On this hand, you have no extras and would double 5S. But note that if partner had had something like ♠x ♥KQx ♦Axx ♣AKxxxx, he might well bid the cold 6C.

With this partnership agreement, if the opponents psyche 4N against you in a competitive auction, it often helps you more than hurts you.

F-12 WALTZING MATILDA

Rubber Bridge (Chicago)	Both Vulnerable		
East Holds: ♠ xxx			
♥ KQJxxxxx			
♦ x			
♣ x			
South Holds: ♠ Axx			
♥ x			
♦ J109x			
♣ AJ9xx			
The Bidding: 1N	2C	X	P
P	2D	X	P
P	2H	P	P
X	P	P	P

You probably looked at the bidding and wondered what was happening here! The East hand holding an eight card heart suit overcalled (bluffed – expecting to get doubled) a natural 2C on his singleton! The South hand looking at AJ98x of clubs after his partner had opened with a strong 1N thought that Christmas had come early. He doubled the vulnerable opponent thinking that it was too good to be true. It was.

Then East, the 2C overcaller, ran to 2D, his other singleton – probably after a slight hesitation and/or other theatrics. South doubled again with his J109x of diamonds planning to lead a trump.

But then East ran again to a third suit, which just happened to be South's singleton. Perhaps South should have smelled a rat! South passed the 2H bid around to his partner who had opened the strong 1N holding A10x in the heart suit. Since his partner had just made two penalty doubles, this was clearly a forcing auction. Unfortunately for him, he chose to double 2H thinking that a trump lead and continuation would leave many losers in the minors.

He was very wrong. The 2H contract made, doubled into game, for a huge money swing. North-South should have bid the vulnerable 3N game which was cold for ten top tricks.

Although North and South were victimized by foxy East, North's double of 2H is highly questionable. Since South was known to be short in hearts – he chose to pass 2H – North should have realized that the opponents had at least an eight card fit. And it is well accepted that you should not double opponents at a low level when they are known to have a good fit (eight cards or more), unless you have four good trumps or more.

No discussion of bluffing at bridge would be complete without including this type of situation. When an opponent bids a suit, gets doubled and then runs, that should raise at least a small question mark in your mind. But then if his second suit gets doubled and he runs to yet a third suit, it may well turn out to be the old-fashion waltz, as in this hand.

This hand also illustrates a concept know as the gratuitous bid. Back in the early days of bridge, when making deceptive bids was much more emphasized than today, it was considered fairly routine to occasionally throw in an extra bid on your way to game. For example, if you opened 1S and your partner raised to 2S, and you intended to bid 4S, you might first bid three of whatever suit that you didn't want led.

These anti-lead directors and other gratuitous inhibiting bids, such as the psychic bidding of short suits as in this given hand, were all yet another colorful aspect of the gamesmanship prevalent in those times. And it was not uncommon for newspapers to carry detailed accounts of some cleverly deceptive bridge bid made by bridge celebrities, such as Eli Culbertson and his wife, Josephine, whose picture graces a wall in The Library of Congress.

F-13 CAKE WALK

MATCHPOINTS	Neither Vulnerable
You Hold: ♠ **KQ109xxxxxx**	
♥ --	
♦ **xx**	
♣ **A**	
The Bidding: 1H	**??**

What would you do with this hand?

In poker, when you are fortunate enough to pick up a super hand, you really should try to make the most of it. Similarly, in bridge, when you pick up a freak hand that can make a game on distribution alone, you really should try to bid the hand artfully – and perhaps get doubled as a bonus.

When I picked up this hand back in the 80s, my first inclination was to trap pass and then come in later perhaps over four hearts. But, of course, that would clearly arouse suspicion. I decided to take the slow approach (*Cross Reference: see C1*), of bidding a mere 1S so that when I came alive later and bid 4S, it might sound like I was saving.

I was a bit worried that what happened to Ron Anderson in a national pairs event might happen to me. Ron was attempting to walk a hand where he held eight solid hearts and some other cards by overcalling a mere 1H. Much to his chagrin, the opponents, who apparently were intimidated by him, chose to pass it out. At least we all had a good laugh.

The auction went according to plan. The left hand opponent (LHO) bid 2S, cue bid in support of hearts, and the opening bidder jumped to 4H. I mustered up all my courage and bid 4S. Without batting an eyebrow the LHO jumped to 6H!

Since he didn't even think about bidding Blackwood, I assumed that he was indeed void in spades. The bidding was passed around back to me. What would you do with this hand now? Although I had an ace, I obviously did not like my defensive potential, but my partner might have a trick, perhaps even a trump trick.

Nevertheless, I decided to take out insurance by accepting a small minus just in case they could make the confident bid of 6H. I bid 6S. LHO passed.

The opening bidder correctly interpreted his partner's pass as an invitation to bid seven – and he did! I quickly doubled 7H and the LHO said, "Uh oh!" I led my ace of clubs for down one doubled and a good score.

F-14 THE ULTIMATE PREEMPT

MPs	Not Vulnerable vs. Vulnerable
You hold: ♠ xx	
♥ xxx	
♦ 10XXX	
♣ AKQ10	
The Bidding: P P ??	

What call would you make with this hand?

Especially at match points, I like the super aggressive poker-style 3C bid here much better than a run-of-the-mill, boring 1C third-hand light opening bid!

Why give the opponents a free ride over your one-club bid which not only takes away no bidding space, but also actually helps your opponents pinpoint their weakness and also gives them a convenient cue-bid. They might have room to find and play game in a four-three major fit instead of no-trump which could easily be a match-point disaster for you.

Generally, all of the reasons given in Aggressive hand A-9, "The Five-card Suit Preempt" also apply to this ultimately short four-card preempt. And let me go on record as definitely recommending against an even more ultimate three-card suit preempt (for example, ace-king-queen)! I seriously believe that would be stretching the principle too far!

Time to fess up. I have specified this particular hand as a match point problem, since it is well recognized that it is sound to occasionally step out of line at match points. Match points, especially at the expert level, is often a wild and wooly game.

But I actually held this hand at IMPs in a Swiss Team event. And notwithstanding the risk of my teammates being very upset with me if my bid backfired (and I went for a big number), I actually chose to bid 3C with this hand! Note well that I would only attempt this madness at IMPs when in third seat and not vulnerable versus vulnerable!

The auction proceeded double, five-clubs by my trusting partner. As my right hand opponent hesitated in deep thought, I realized that I could be in big trouble. As it turned out however, although my partner had very few high card points, he had just the right shape hand for me (3-1-5-4), and I might well have only gone down minus five-hundred at the five level.

My right hand opponent, looking at three little clubs in his hand, assumed that his partner would have a singleton or void club, and decided to bid six-hearts. Although the dummy came down with seventeen points, it had two clubs. I was able to cash out for down one - a great result for us. And, my teammates did not complain at all about my ultimate preempt!

F-15 THE STRIPED-TAIL APE DOUBLE

MATCHPOINTS	Vulnerable vs. Non Vulnerable
You Hold: ♠ QJ10xxx ♥ AQ10x ♦ KQJ ♣ -- [BW 600]	
The Bidding: 1S 4C 4S X ??	

What call would you make with this hand? Would you ever dream of doubling??

Oh yes! What would the world be like without color? Every now and then, we all see something new and different – and sometimes strange, at the poker table or bridge table. Here is a most colorful ploy that you should know about.

But to be in the properly receptive mode, imagine that your Amazon Jungle safari comes upon a clearing where the natives, schooled by English missionaries, are holding a duplicate tournament at tea time. It could happen! While touring the papal palaces in Avignon, we once came upon a duplicate tournament in progress.

John Lowenthal fantasized that he held the above hand while playing against native tribesmen who apparently had developed a number of rather advanced bridge techniques. He passed the penalty double, perhaps assuming that his partner might have stretched. But a fine dummy appeared – actually, much too fine! He had no trouble taking all the tricks, plus 1390, for a match point zero – since all the other pairs bid at least the small slam with his cards. Thus, the double, instead of being a gratuity, turned out to be a dastardly trick!

In the post mortem, when he decided in retrospect that he should have redoubled, the natives replied, "We call this Striped Tail Ape Double, because we run from redouble – zoom, like striped tail ape." Thus, the concept and the name were coined back in the 60s.

SEQUEL

In the middle 70s, while playing with my first wife, Kathie, on our way to one of our back-to-back second-place finishes in the Blue-Ribbon Pairs, a hand occurred where I was using Blackwood in a slam auction. I had bid 4N and Kathie had shown the missing ace. I bid 5N asking for kings when Tony Dionesi, my left hand opponent, doubled! Kathie passed, which showed one-king.

I had to sit and think about the scoring. If I passed 5N doubled and made an overtrick, that would certainly score less than bidding slam. Redoubling with a 400 point overtrick would be more than a small slam. I redoubled, and Tony ran, like a Striped Tail Ape to 6C, the suit which his partner had preempted. Since I was pretty sure that the save would only go for five or six tricks, I bid the 6N which made. As I left his table, we both had a good chuckle when I offered to buy him a banana.

F-16 FRIENDS AND COMPETITORS

IMPs	Not Vulnerable vs. Vulnerable
You Hold:	♠ x
	♥ Q9xxx
	♦ 10xxx
	♣ J9x
The Bidding:	3C 3D ??

What call would you make with this hand?

This hand occurred in a Swiss team event at the Ocean City Regional (Maryland) in October, 2003, while I was in the process of writing this book. My Canadian partner, George Colter, usually makes sound preempts. Our opponents were old friends, a married couple who had moved from the Washington, D.C. area to North Carolina. Peggy Allen, also from the Washington area was kibitzing me. Since we all knew each other well, a very friendly and congenial atmosphere prevailed at the table.

My first inclination was to simply bid 5C. Perhaps then I could have used this hand in Section A. However, a fiendish urge came over me, possessed me momentarily, and I found myself bidding 3N!

My left hand opponent with eight high card points had no clear bid. From her perspective, I might well have had a legitimate 3N bid, so she passed. If she had doubled on points, assuming her partner had an opening bid for his 3D overcall, and led a diamond, I might very well win the diamond and run seven clubs and another trick.

Of course, if I was doubled, I planned to run to four clubs even faster than the striped-tail ape (see previous hand)! We ended the hand down two, undoubled (minus 100), whereas our partners at the other table were making the vulnerable game in spades for a pickup of eleven IMPs.

When the hand was over, Peggy nudged me and said, "Oh, you are very tricky." My friends from North Carolina were very good natured about it; they are both seasoned players and understand the ferocity of bridge competition.

This rather recent hand certainly exemplifies some of the wonderfully colorful and deceptive poker-like bids that often occur in bridge at the expert levels. More importantly it exemplifies, the "all in good fun" spirit.

F-17 A RECENT ILLUSION OF STRENGTH

IMPs	Neither Vulnerable [Orlando Regional 2004]
You Hold:	♠ Q10xxx ♥ AJ ♦ Jx ♣ J10xx
Bidding: 2S P ??	

About three months after writing the preceding article, Friends and Competitors, I ran into an old friend, Arnie Fisher, who held this hand while playing in a regional knock out event against Jeff Meckstroth and Eric Rodwell, who are arguably the best partnership in the world, and also the most successful in recent years.

Although most players would raise to three or four spades with this hand, Arnie decided to have a little fun with his esteemed opponents and created an illusion of strength by bidding 3N!!* His opponents might well be on for a game and his left hand opponent certainly must have at least an opening bid. 3N was passed out and Arnie was rather surprised to see a dummy that some would consider an opening (one) bid. Dummy was ♠KJxxxx ♥Kxx ♦Kx ♣xx. Note that many modern experts play that there is no hand that is too good for a weak two-bid but not good enough for an opening one-bid.

A heart was led from Q10xx won by Arnie's jack. Arnie played a small spade to the king, losing to the ace. Right hand opponent continued with hearts to Arnie's ace. Arnie was now at another cross road.

Arnie could cash eight tricks for down one, which would be the same result as 3S if the king of diamonds was offside. If both the ace and queen of diamonds was offside, then the opponent could make 4H. But the bidding indicated that Arnie's left hand opponent held more than half of the missing twenty-one points, and right-hand opponent had already showed the ace of spades.

So Arnie decided to go for it and try to get the ninth trick with the king of diamonds. He led the jack of diamonds, which was more likely to get ducked. Sure enough, left hand opponent ducked smoothly and Arnie called for the king – and scored up 3N. Note that the opponents could have cashed out five top tricks at any time if they knew the situation.

* When I was an MIT student learning to play bridge at the Boston Chess Club, an elderly lady called Fifi (Harding) successfully psyched 3N after her partner's preempt. She later told me that she had learned to create an illusion of strength from Dorothy Sims (wife of P. Hal Sims).